"America's public parks are beloved and widely : National parks have even been called 'America's the story? In *Violent and Verdant*, KangJae Lee such unquestioning reverence. Presenting both deep community and urban parks, state parks, and nat the displacement, discrimination, and disenfranchisement that has often accompanied park creation and management. To resist such injustice, Lee provides insights into the strategies elites employ to direct the benefits of public parks to themselves and recommends counterstrategies to oppose them. If you are involved with America's public parks, you do not want to miss *Violent and Verdant*."

Terence G. Young, *Professor Emeritus of Geography and Anthropology, California Polytechnic University, Pomona*

"With the publication of *Violent and Verdant*, Professor Lee positions himself as one of the most important critical voices on the social construction and contestation of parks in America. His book is singular in applying an unflinching social justice perspective to the full scale of the park movement—from city and state parks to our heavily visited and often romanticized national parks. While Lee persuasively documents the under-discussed role of capitalism, oppression, elitism, and violence in the origin and development of parks, he also writes the badly needed story of marginalized groups resisting this injustice. Lee's conclusions are brilliantly sobering: if we want parks to be truly democratic spaces in the future, we must reform structural inequalities, not just in parks but within the wider society. *Violence and Verdant* should be essential reading for researchers and teachers in various fields, park managers and advocates, and many park visitors. Lee's monograph is a welcomed challenge to the political times in which we find ourselves as educational and public discussions of America's white supremacist foundations are discouraged, if not banned outright."

Derek H. Alderman, *Professor of Geography, University of Tennessee*

"In this groundbreaking book, social scientist KangJae Lee offers a compelling analysis of the complex history of U.S. public parks, showing how these highly valued public spaces, often seen as symbols of democracy and egalitarianism, have been sites of systemic racial injustice. Drawing on interdisciplinary research, he documents well how public parks have historically reinforced the racial hierarchy, benefiting whites at the expense of communities of color. He challenges us to rethink the societal role of public parks and seek a more just and inclusive future for them. His scholarship is timely and highly original, providing critical insights into the intersections of environmental justice with systemic racism. A must-read book for all interested in understanding the social justice dynamics of U.S. public spaces."

Joe R. Feagin, *Distinguished Professor (emeritus), Texas A&M University, and author of* The White Racial Frame *(2nd edn, Routledge, 2020)*

Violent and Verdant

Public parks in the U.S. are one of the most contentious and paradoxical places. Many Americans believe public parks are encapsulations of nature, promoters of health, and embodiments of egalitarianism and democracy, providing a wide range of health, economic, cultural, and social benefits to users. Yet, the historical reality of American public parks has been riddled with greed, hypocrisy, prejudice, and ulterior motives of the rich and powerful. Numerous people have been displaced, exploited, and even killed because of public parks.

Drawing from multiple disciplines such as sociology, history, geography, urban planning, environmental science, and leisure studies, *Violent and Verdant: Systemic Injustice in Public Parks in the U.S.* takes a two-pronged approach to provide critical and fresh insights on public parks in the U.S. It looks back, illuminating how parks have been sites of enduring violence and oppression. But it also looks forward, offering practical strategies and philosophical reimaginations of parks' conception, development, and management.

KangJae Jerry Lee is Assistant Professor in the Department of Parks, Recreation, & Tourism at the University of Utah. He is an interdisciplinary researcher on social and environmental justice, race and ethnicity, outdoor recreation, and subjective wellbeing. His research and teaching have been recognized by several awards, including the Opal Mann Green Engagement and Scholarship Award from North Carolina State University, the Best Research Paper Award from the Academy of Leisure Sciences, the Golden Apple Award in Excellent Teaching and Mentorship at the University of Missouri.

New Critical Viewpoints on Society Series
Edited by Joe R. Feagin

Who Killed Higher Education?
Maintaining White Dominance in a Desegregation Era
Edna B. Chun and Joe R. Feagin

The Spanish Language in the United States
Racialization, Rootedness, and Resistance
Edited by José A. Cobas, Bonnie Urciuoli, Joe R. Feagin, and Daniel J. Delgado

Indian, Black and Irish
Indigenous Nations, African Peoples, European Invasions – 1492–1790
James V. Fenelon

Kindness Wars
The History of Political Economy of Human Caring
Noel A. Cazenave

Recolonizing Africa
An Ethnography of Land Acquisition, Mining, and Resource Control
Mariam Mniga

Race, Class, Gender, and the Struggle for Social Justice in Higher Education
Unveiling the Unnamed Elite
Angela D. Calise

Violent and Verdant
Systemic Injustice in Public Parks in the U.S.
KangJae Jerry Lee

For more information about this series, please visit:
www.routledge.com/New-Critical-Viewpoints-on-Society/book-series/NCVS

Violent and Verdant
Systemic Injustice in Public Parks in the U.S.

KangJae Jerry Lee

NEW YORK AND LONDON

Designed cover image: Shutterstock

First published 2025
by Routledge
605 Third Avenue, New York, NY 10158

and by Routledge
4 Park Square, Milton Park, Abingdon, Oxon, OX14 4RN

Routledge is an imprint of the Taylor & Francis Group, an informa business

© 2025 KangJae Jerry Lee

The right of KangJae Jerry Lee to be identified as author of this work has been asserted in accordance with sections 77 and 78 of the Copyright, Designs and Patents Act 1988.

All rights reserved. No part of this book may be reprinted or reproduced or utilised in any form or by any electronic, mechanical, or other means, now known or hereafter invented, including photocopying and recording, or in any information storage or retrieval system, without permission in writing from the publishers.

Trademark notice: Product or corporate names may be trademarks or registered trademarks, and are used only for identification and explanation without intent to infringe.

ISBN: 9781032707617 (hbk)
ISBN: 9781032661926 (pbk)
ISBN: 9781032707624 (ebk)

DOI: 10.4324/9781032707624

Typeset in Sabon
by Newgen Publishing UK

To my father, Jung-Hee Lee, who taught me how to *fight*.

To my mother, Jong-Pal Kim, who taught me how to *love*.

To my wife, So-Yon An, who taught me how to *balance*.

Contents

Acknowledgements   *x*

Introduction   1

PART I   11

1 Community and Urban Parks   13

2 State Parks   34

3 National Parks   61

PART II   87

4 Systemic Park Injustice and the People's Resistance   89

5 Creating Democratic Parks in an Undemocratic Nation?   116

Index   *135*

Acknowledgements

I am deeply grateful to John Heffernan and the Foundation for Systemic Change. Without their generous support and encouragement, this work would not have been possible.

My scholarly foundation was built at the Department of Recreation, Park, & Tourism Sciences at Texas A&M University. I was fortunate to learn from David Scott, Jim Gramann, Corliss Outley, Gary Ellis, and Mike Edwards.

I could not have come this far without the teaching and mentoring from Joe Feagin at Texas A&M. His books and classes profoundly changed the way I see the world.

I am thankful for Myron Floyd, Monika Stodolska, and Rod Dieser. I have been fortunate to learn from and collaborate with some of the best researchers in leisure studies.

I am grateful for the encouragement, shared knowledge, and intellectual inspirations from Rasul Mowatt and Corey Johnson.

Special thanks to Clarence Jefferson Hall Jr. and Justin Harmon for their meticulous reviews of my manuscripts. Their insights and expert knowledge have made this book much stronger.

I want to acknowledge the technical support from Alfred Mowdood and other librarians at the University of Utah. Their assistance with book contracts, citation management, and archival research made this book project a lot smoother.

Finally, I extend my gratitude to Susanna Klingenberg and Michael Gibson. Their reviews and edits have made this book eminently more readable.

Introduction

A very great number of poor families who worked a number of years on these [lots], squatters and leaseground, will be entirely ruined when they must give up their cultivated land and move away without compensation. Please to have mercy on the Poor, then the Lord will have mercy with you.
Jupiter Zeuss Hesser[1]

Chief Mountain is my head. Now my head is cut off. The mountains have been my last refuge…Now, we will sell you the mountain portion of our land and we will make a good treaty, but in the future we don't want our Great Father to ask for anything more. We don't want our land allotted.
Chief White Calf[2]

The sign said, "Jones Lake State Park. Negroes Only." That was out by the road. I would have to go to Jones Lake and you would have been going to White Lake … . See, at White Lake, there were places where you could go and spend the night. And there were places where you could go inside and dance and eat. But we didn't have anything like that at Jones Lake. So whenever integration came about, people started going to White Lake.
Sallie Powell[3]

These voices speak from the past, but their struggles and suffering echo loudly through time. But, what is the source of their agony exactly? Hesser received an eviction order in 1855, along with many other working-class people, to clear the land that would eventually become New York City's Central Park. He pleaded with the city government to provide fair monetary compensation for the land that he and his neighbors had to give up.[4]

White Calf was chief of the Blackfeet in Montana. In his response to the 1895 Agreement which ceded a western portion of the Blackfeet Indian Reservation to the U.S. government, White Calf defended the Chief Mountain, or Ninastako, the sacred place for the Blackfeet. His likening of the reservation to a tribal body and the agreement to a beheading of his people demonstrates just how deeply felt these land losses were. Fifteen years

DOI: 10.4324/9781032707624-1

after the agreement, the lands ceded by the Blackfeet became the eastern half of Glacier National Park.[5]

Sallie Powell was an African American mathematics teacher in Elizabethtown, North Carolina. While Powell reflected on her loving memories on Jones Lake State Park, the first segregated state park in North Carolina established in 1939, she also shared her sorrowful memories of its inadequate infrastructure and lack of indoor facilities compared to White Lake. Until 1965, Jones Lake was one of only two state parks available for African Americans in North Carolina.[6]

It is their stories—and stories like theirs—that have been marginalized for too long. Hesser, White Calf, and Powell lived in different times and locations, yet they all suffered from displacement, discrimination, and disenfranchisement because of *public parks*. Public parks built for the enrichment of our lives were in fact created by destroying the lives of so many people. This book will bring to light this paradoxical and uncomfortable history behind American public parks and look forward with a critical eye to their future.

Many Americans have a hard time connecting public parks with struggles and suffering, because parks are portrayed as a positive part of the nation's history and even core identity. Regardless of their variations in the design, size, and location, public parks in the U.S. are essentially tax-funded environmental infrastructures owned and operated by government sectors for the benefit of all taxpayers. Since they are fundamentally public amenities, public parks have historically been touted as democratic, egalitarian, and salubrious.

For instance, when park pioneers started to build community and urban parks in major American cities in the mid to late 1800s, public parks were advocated as an encapsulation of nature, democratic leisure space, and an antidote to various urban problems such as population density, air pollution, and even cultural and moral degradation.[7] Since their inception in the late 1800s, national parks have been described as the "crown jewels" of America and "America's best idea" capturing the American imagination and inspiring patriotism via pristine wilderness.[8] Similarly, when state parks started to emerge during the late 1800s and early 1900s, they were advocated as natural recreation settings that "cure the ills of society" and promote a healthier and happier citizenry.[9] Whether it is a small community park, a magnificent national park, or a state park in between, the refrain echoes through the country's history that public parks are places to cherish for respite, joy, health, and happiness.

This positive image has been backed up with volumes of empirical studies highlighting various benefits of public parks. Studies have found that community and urban parks promote physical activity and mental health among nearby residents and function as a buffer against environmental problems, such as heat islands and air pollution.[10] National parks not only preserve millions of acres of natural environment from commercial development, but also serve as some of the most popular travel destinations in the nation. State park systems generate 2.2 billion hours of nature recreation and more than a billion dollars of revenue annually.[11] Today, public parks in the U.S. are recognized as indispensable environmental amenities for a variety of health, economic, cultural, and social benefits.[12]

Yet, the historical reality of public parks is far more peculiar. A critical review of the birth and the developmental process of community and urban parks, state parks, and national parks since the mid-1800s illustrates profound disjunction from the utopian image many Americans have of parks. The unscrupulous scheming that led to our now-beloved parks goes back to their very beginnings.

When the United States went through rapid industrialization and urbanization during the 1800s, White urban elites started to campaign for creating urban space called "parks." Impressed by newly created public parks in Europe, American urban elites desired to create similar space(s) in their home country. They advocated that parks could serve as elixirs of health, solving urban problems and creating democratic leisure space where people from all walks of life could recreate and relax. Yet, contrary to their claims, the main beneficiaries of urban parks were affluent and influential White individuals, people like themselves: they profited from the real estate development, and the parks were frequently built far away from working-class communities.[13] Moreover, some elites built public parks with a more overtly sinister motive: They methodically used park development to demolish communities of color or demarcate and reinforce residential racial segregation.[14]

National parks are the domestic emblems of American imperialism and settler colonialism as well as White conservation leaders' desire to protect American wilderness, in part, for the prosperity of the White race. The United States acquired vast wildlands in the West through colonial conquest and ethnic cleansing against Indigenous peoples, as well as extortion of their lands through wars and fraudulent treaties.[15] White conservation leaders designated some of the newly acquired lands as national parks, a seemingly beneficent act for nature conservation. However, fueling their motivation was avarice for profits through railroad expansion and tourism development.[16] Another distinctive motive was White supremacists' desire to preserve White dominance in the nation. This could be done, they believed, if White Americans frequented rugged natural areas to strengthen their health and to cultivate masculine character through hunting, fishing, and quasi-military explorations.[17] Further, to entice more tourists, the newly established national parks in the West were advertised as "untouched" or "virgin" lands, as if no human civilization ever existed there. Concomitantly, the Indigenous culture was heavily exploited in the marketing aimed at tourists. Once established, what prevailed in national parks were Eurocentric elitist conservation rules which criminalized the hunting and fishing practices of Indigenous peoples and the working-class as overexploitation of wildlife.[18]

The troubling history trickled down to the state park era. When the creation of the National Park System gave momentum to the state park movement during the first half of the 1900s, the U.S. was in the middle of Jim Crow era. The "separate but equal" law was firmly entrenched in the Southern states, yet it was also a common cultural norm throughout Northern states.[19] Through the National Conference on Parks held in Des Moines, Iowa in 1921, state park leaders in the nation developed a bold vision to create at least one state park within 100 miles driving for all Americans.[20] Yet, Jim Crow laws and customs did not allow African Americans to visit state parks with Whites. The former had to use segregated park facilities called "Negro Areas" that were rare and usually in poor condition. Furthermore, it is a sad irony that many of the state parks unavailable to African Americans were built or renovated by African Americans who were members of the Civilian Conservation Corps during the Great Depression.[21]

Thus, the parks in which Americans love and take pride were in fact built on an ideological foundation of capitalism, colonialism, elitism, eugenics, imperialism, racism, and xenophobia. Since their inception, public parks in the U.S. have been conceptualized, built, and managed by affluent and powerful White individuals in order to gain economic benefits via real estate and commercial development, create White recreational spaces, instill White middle- and upper-class values on others, preserve White supremacy, and Americanize immigrants. They built parks by committing genocide against the Indigenous peoples, displacing the poor and people of color, and excluding and exploiting African Americans. Even though many people perceive parks as an encapsulation of nature, a promoter of health, and an embodiment of egalitarianism and democracy, the historical reality is that so many people have been deceived, exploited, displaced, and even killed because of public parks. From this perspective, public parks are one of the most contentious and paradoxical pieces of American geography.

Unfortunately, this dark history of American public parks is not a distant past, but *an ongoing reality*. Studies have documented that parks in communities of color and low-income groups tend to be less prevalent, smaller, underfunded, crowded, and unsafe compared to those in middle- and upper-class White communities.[22] New parks projects meant to address the park disparities often trigger environmental gentrification and displace local residents who are supposed to be the main beneficiaries.[23] In state and national parks, people of color often constitute only a fraction of the total visitors, because they experience far more financial, cultural, and social barriers compared to their White counterparts, all of which are closely tied to centuries of systematic and institutional discrimination against people of color.[24] Moreover, people of color frequently experience racial discrimination within public parks, and their mere presence and recreational activities are routinely criminalized by White police and park users.[25]

At the heart of American parks, then, is *a contradiction*—the conspicuous gap between what park leaders promised to the people and what actually happened during and after park developments. Pioneers of community and urban parks promised that parks would bring social and cultural advancement. But whose idea of advancement was legitimized and actualized? Who, precisely, prospered? American conservation leaders created national parks to prevent environmental destruction and overexploitation of natural resources. But at what cost to numerous human lives? State officials developed state park systems to generate tourism revenue and provide wholesome recreation for all Americans. But what was their definition of "Americans" exactly? The paradoxes surrounding American public parks are seemingly endless.

How should we make sense of these alarming discrepancies? On the one hand, they certainly appear to be a series of meticulously crafted false promises or deceptive narratives from the White ruling class for the purpose of taking advantage of the parks and the people. After all, the history of American public parks is riddled with greed, hypocrisy, prejudice, and ulterior motives of the rich and powerful. On the other hand, the discrepancies exhibit distinctive parallels with the social stratification and polarization that stubbornly persist across different times and locations of human history: privileged groups continue to be privileged or become even more privileged, whereas underprivileged groups remain vulnerable or become further marginalized. In this reading of history, public parks serve as a microcosm of human society, offering poignant representations of our avarice and struggles for possession, power, and control. American public parks deeply intersect with some of the most consistent patterns of human affairs—and the most distressing.

What is to be done about this troubling history of American public parks? This book attempts to address this simple yet arduous question. Drawing from multiple disciplines such as sociology, history, geography, urban planning, environmental science, and leisure studies, I offer greater detail about the complex, uncomfortable, yet compelling stories of the past, present, and future of American public parks. By doing so, I aim to give voice to unheard people, challenge and disrupt our evangelical views on public parks, and offer specific recommendations to rectify the centuries of environmental and social injustice surrounding public parks.

Part I provides critical analyses of the history of community, state, and national parks in the United States and illuminates how these supposedly democratic and inclusive spaces have, in fact, been sites of enduring violence and oppression. Chapter 1 begins with the early history of Boston Common and Central Park, illustrating the ways in which park pioneers historically used their means and power to create community and urban parks at the expense of the lives and well-being of the working-class, immigrants, and people of color. Chapter 2 excavates colonialist, imperialist, and capitalist ideologies embedded in the two earliest state parks, Indian Springs in Georgia and Yosemite in California. The second half of the chapter examines the stark contrast between the democratic ideals underpinning the state park movement during the first half of the 20th century and the racial discrimination in state parks that excluded generations of African Americans. Chapter 3 delves into the elitism, racism, and sexism in the American conservation movement that propelled the creation of U.S. national parks. It also reviews the birth of Yellowstone in the West and Great Smoky Mountains and Shenandoah National Parks in the East, highlighting that these parks could not have been established without the settler colonialism and capitalist avarice that forcibly displaced Indigenous peoples and working-class Appalachian residents.

Part II focuses on the present and future of American public parks. Chapter 4 offers an overarching review of systemic park injustice in American public parks and how ordinary people have fought against it. It offers a formal conceptualization of systemic park injustice and summarizes 14 specific strategies that the White ruling class employed in order to benefit from public parks. It also summarizes 13 counterstrategies that vulnerable and marginalized groups have used to fight against park injustice. Chapter 5 situates systemic park injustice within a broader historical and ideological context of the United States. It illustrates that the democratic ideals of public parks are very difficult to achieve because parks rest on an undemocratic American society. In this macro-level analysis, I draw from Marxist critiques of capitalism and make suggestions for a democratic future of American society and its public parks.

Notes

1 Roy Rosenzweig and Elizabeth Blackmar, *The Park and the People: A History of Central Park* (Cornell University Press, 1998), 84.
2 "No. 118, 54th Congress., 1st Session., (Feb. 12, 1896)." https://shareok.org/bitstream/handle/11244/35526/Senate-54-1-Document-118-Serial-3350.pdf?sequence=1&isAllowed=y., 19 Senate Document. No. 118, 54th Congress., 1st Session., (Feb. 12, 1896). Retrieved from https://shareok.org/bitstream/handle/11244/35526/Senate-54-1-Document-118-Serial-3350.pdf?sequence=1&isAllowed=y
3 David Cecelski, "Listening to History (Sallie Powell: Mr. Dewitt's Lake)," *The News & Observer* April 29 2007 https://www.ncpedia.org/listening-to-history/powell-sallie-0.
4 Rosenzweig and Blackmar, *The Park and the People*.
5 Mark David Spence, *Dispossessing the Wilderness: Indian Removal and the Making of the National Parks* (Oxford University Press, 1999); David R. Craig, Laurie Yung, and William T. Borrie, "'Blackfeet Belong to the Mountains': Hope, Loss, and Blackfeet Claims to Glacier National Park, Montana," *Conservation and Society* 10, no. 3 (2012).
6 William E. O'Brien, *Landscapes of Exclusion: State Parks and Jim Crow in the American South* (University of Massachusetts Press, 2015).
7 Galen Cranz, *The Politics of Park Design: A History of Urban Parks in America* (MIT Press, 1982); Kevin Loughran, "Urban parks and urban problems: An historical perspective on green space development as a cultural fix," *Urban Studies* 57, no. 11 (2018), https://doi.org/10.1177/0042098018763555; Rosenzweig and Blackmar, *The Park and the People*.
8 Lary M. Dilsaver, *America's National Park System: The Critical Documents* (Rowman & Littlefield, 2016); Alfred Runte, *National Parks: The American Experience* (University of Nebraska Press, 1997).
9 Langdon Smith, "Democratizing nature through state park development," *Historical Geography* 41 (2013).
10 Lincoln R. Larson, Viniece Jennings, and Scott A. Cloutier, "Public parks and wellbeing in urban areas of the United States," *PLoS one* 11, no. 4 (2016); Jasper Schipperijn et al., "Access to parks and physical activity: An eight country comparison," *Urban Forestry & Urban Greening* 27 (2017).
11 Juha Siikamäki, "Contributions of the US state park system to nature recreation," *Proceedings of the National Academy of Sciences* 108, no. 34 (2011); J. W. Smith, E. J. Wilkins, and Y. F. Leung, "Attendance trends threaten future operations of America's state park systems," *PNAS* 116, no. 26 (Jun 25 2019).
12 Ariane L. Bedimo-Rung, Andrew J. Mowen, and Deborah A. Cohen, "The significance of parks to physical activity and public health: a conceptual model," *American Journal of Preventive Medicine* 28, no. 2 (2005); Cecil C. Konijnendijk et al., *Benefits of Urban Parks: A Systematic Review*, A Report for IFPRA, Copenhagen & Alnarp, 2013.
13 Michael Rawson, *Eden on the Charles: The Making of Boston* (Harvard University Press, 2010); Rosenzweig and Blackmar, *The Park and the People*; Dorceta E. Taylor, "Central Park as a model for social control: urban parks, social class and leisure behavior in nineteenth-century America," *Journal of Leisure Research* 31, no. 4 (1999).

8 Violent and Verdant

14 Stephen R. Hausmann, "Erasing Indian Country: Urban Native Space and the 1972 Rapid City Flood," *Western Historical Quarterly* 52, no. 3 (2021); Kevin Loughran, *Parks for Profit: Selling Nature in the City* (Columbia University Press, 2022); Antero Pietila, *Not in My Neighborhood: How Bigotry Shaped a Great American City* (Rowman & Littlefield, 2012).

15 Vine Deloria and Raymond J. DeMallie, *Documents of American Indian Diplomacy: Treaties, Agreements, and Conventions, 1775–1979* (University of Oklahoma Press, 1999); Roxanne Dunbar-Ortiz, *An Indigenous Peoples' History of the United States* (Beacon Press, 2014); Isaac Kantor, "Ethnic cleansing and America's creation of national parks," *Public Land & Resources Law Review* 28 (2007).

16 Mark Daniel Barringer, *Selling Yellowstone: Capitalism and the Construction of Nature* (University Press of Kansas, 2002); Margaret Lynn Brown, "Captains of Tourism: Selling a National Park in the Great Smoky Mountains," *Journal of the Appalachian Studies Association* 4 (1992); Daniel Smith Pierce, *Boosters, Bureaucrats, Politicians and philanthropists: Coalition Building in the Establishment of the Great Smoky Mountains National Park* (The University of Tennessee, 1995); Dennis E. Simmons, "Conservation, cooperation, and controversy: The establishment of Shenandoah National Park, 1924–1936," *The Virginia Magazine of History and Biography* (1981).

17 Gary Gerstle, "Theodore Roosevelt and the divided character of American nationalism," *The Journal of American History* 86, no. 3 (1999); KangJae Jerry Lee et al., "Slow violence in public parks in the U.S.: can we escape our troubling past?" *Social & Cultural Geography* 24, no. 7 (2023), https://doi.org/10.1080/14649 365.2022.2028182; Carolyn Merchant, "Shades of darkness: Race and environmental history," *Environmental History* 8, no. 3 (2003); Rasul A. Mowatt, "A People's History of Leisure Studies: The Great Race and the National Parks and U.S. Forests," *Journal of Park and Recreation Administration* 38, no. 3 (2020); Miles A. Powell, *Vanishing America: Species Extinction, Racial Peril, and the Origins of Conservation* (Harvard University Press, 2016); Dorceta E. Taylor, *The Rise of the American Conservation Movement: Power, Privilege, and Environmental Protection* (Duke University Press, 2016).

18 For the marketing of Indigenous culture, see Spence, *Dispossessing the Wilderness*. For the criminalization in hunting and fishing, see Karl Jacoby, *Crimes against Nature: Squatters, Poachers, Thieves, and the Hidden History of American Conservation* (University of California Press, 2014).

19 Joe R. Feagin, *Systemic Racism: A Theory of Oppression* (New York: Routledge, 2006); Gary B. Nash, *Race and Revolution* (Rowman & Littlefield, 1990).

20 Rebecca Conard, "The National Conference on State Parks: Reflections on Organizational Genealogy" (paper presented at the The George Wright Forum, 1997), 34, 36; Ney C. Landrum, *The State Park Movement in America: A Critical Review* (University of Missouri Press, 2004), Chapter 6; Freeman Tilden, *The State Parks: Their Meaning in American Life* (Alfred A. Knopf, 1962), 8.

21 William E. O'Brien, "State parks and Jim Crow in the decade before Brown v. Board of Education," *Geographical Review* 102, no. 2 (2012); O'Brien, *Landscapes of Exclusion*. James Wright Steely, *Parks for Texas: Enduring Landscapes of the New Deal* (University of Texas Press, 2010).

22 Jason Byrne, Jennifer Wolch, and Jin Zhang, "Planning for environmental justice in an urban national park," *Journal of Environmental Planning and Management*

52, no. 3 (2009); Alessandro Rigolon, "A complex landscape of inequity in access to urban parks: A literature review," *Landscape and Urban Planning* 153 (2016); Alessandro Rigolon, Matthew Browning, and Viniece Jennings, "Inequities in the quality of urban park systems: An environmental justice investigation of cities in the United States," *Landscape and Urban Planning* 178 (2018); Chona Sister, Jennifer Wolch, and John Wilson, "Got green? Addressing environmental justice in park provision," *GeoJournal* 75, no. 3 (2010); Monika Stodolska et al., "Perceptions of urban parks as havens and contested terrains by Mexican-Americans in Chicago neighborhoods," *Leisure Sciences* 33, no. 2 (2011); Jennifer Wolch, John P. Wilson, and Jed Fehrenbach, "Parks and park funding in Los Angeles: An equity-mapping analysis," *Urban Geography* 26, no. 1 (2005).

23 Kenneth Gould and Tammy Lewis, *Green Gentrification: Urban Sustainability and the Struggle for Environmental Justice* (Routledge, 2016); Loughran, *Parks for Profit*; Hamil Pearsall and Jillian K. Eller, "Locating the green space paradox: A study of gentrification and public green space accessibility in Philadelphia, Pennsylvania," *Landscape and Urban Planning* 195 (2020); Jennifer R. Wolch, Jason Byrne, and Joshua P. Newell, "Urban green space, public health, and environmental justice: The challenge of making cities 'just green enough,'" *Landscape and Urban Planning* 125 (2014).

24 John Burkett, Tim Tyrrell, and Randy Virden, "National Park Service Visitation Trends: Exploring the Forces that Influence Visitation," *National Park Service* (2010); Lee et al., "Slow violence in public parks in the U.S."; KangJae Jerry Lee and David Scott, "Bourdieu and African Americans' Park Visitation: The Case of Cedar Hill State Park in Texas," *Leisure Sciences* 38, no. 5 (2016), https://doi.org/10.1080/01490400.2015.1127188; David Scott and KangJae Jerry Lee, "People of color and their constraints to national parks visitation," *The George Wright Forum* 35, no. 1 (2018).

25 Regina Austin, "Not just for the fun of it: governmental restraints on black leisure, social inequality, and the privatization of public space," *Southern California Law Review* 71 (1998); Sarah Burns, *The Central Park Five: A Chronicle of a City Wilding* (Alfred A. Knopf, 2011); Brandon Harris, Alessandro Rigolon, and Mariela Fernandez, "'To them, we're just kids from the hood: Citizen-based policing of youth of color, 'white space,' and environmental gentrification," *Cities* 107 (2020).

PART I

1 Community and Urban Parks

It is of great importance as the first real park made in this country—a democratic development of the highest significance & on the success of which, in my opinion, much of the progress of art & esthetic culture in this country is dependent.

Fredrick Law Olmsted[1]

Anything that was public was also white. For example, the public park, the public playground, they were white. They had some little Mickey Mouse playgrounds, but they were what they called exclusively colored, as if it were worth being exclusive.

John W. Brown[2]

In a letter to his brother, Fredrick Law Olmsted explained the significance of Central Park as a democratic space and artistic expression of cultural advancement. Olmsted is one of the most important figures in the history of public parks in the United States. Born in an affluent family in Hartford, Connecticut in 1822, Olmsted was exposed to European parks and gardens from his formative years. After he became the superintendent and co-designer of Central Park in the 1850s, the first landscaped public park in the U.S., Olmsted emerged as the most influential park planner in the nation and made profound impacts on the design and management principles of American public parks. Throughout his career, Olmsted advocated parks as a democratic space where social class and inequality could be erased.[3]

Yet, John W. Brown's experience with public parks poignantly contradicts Olmsted's ideas. Growing up in Portsmouth, Virginia during the Jim Crow era, Brown notes that public parks were exclusively for White people. His description is consistent with what many historians have documented. During the first half of the 20th century, public and semi-public recreation facilities such as parks, theaters, billiard clubs, and theme parks were racially segregated or, worse, simply unavailable to people of color because of institutionalized racism.[4]

DOI: 10.4324/9781032707624-3

14 *Violent and Verdant*

The sharp contrast between Olmsted's philosophy and Brown's life experience succinctly captures the most disturbing yet consistent theme in the history of American public parks. Although the notion of democracy, cultural advancement, social progress, and health benefits have been at the heart of American public parks since their inception, the beneficiaries of the parks have been mostly upper- and middle-class White Americans for the past two centuries. Throughout the country's history, the ruling elite have constantly used public parks as a tool to materialize their own interests at the expense of the lives and wellbeing of people with limited means and power. To begin unraveling these contrasting yet deeply intertwined realities captured by Olmsted and Brown, this chapter critically reviews the beginning of community and urban parks in the United States and how they have evolved until today.

The First Community and Urban Parks

The origin of community and urban parks in the United States can be traced back to European urban planning traditions. The Spaniards brought to the New World the concept of the central plaza, a public square in a city or town. The Plaza de la Constitución, originally the Plaza de Armas, in St. Augustine, Florida is one of the earliest examples of public space on American soil that still exists today. Established in 1598 by Gonzalo Mendez de Canzo, the governor of Spanish La Florida, the Plaza followed the planning guidelines outlined in the Spanish Royal Cedulas (ordinances) of 1573. Since its establishment, the Plaza has served as a multipurpose space and focal point of the community where people conducted business, socialized, and held events, celebrations, and military drills.[5]

Similarly, English colonists brought the centuries-old English common land system to the New World. Boston Common was one of several common lands established in New England. Commons, also called "greens," were communal properties that nearby residents could use for grazing animals, catching fish, harvesting edible and medicinal plants, and collecting stones, sand, and firewood.[6] In Old England, the ownership and access rights to commons were somewhat vague because although rural lords or municipalities held title to the common, they usually needed "the consent of the commoners or an Act of Parliament to sell, develop, or cultivate common land."[7] Yet, as early as the 13th century, the common lands were gradually privatized or "enclosed," taking away commoners' rights to use the lands. In New England, common lands were first owned and accessed exclusively by European colonists, yet they were later turned into public space or sold to private entities.[8] Boston Common followed a similar path.

Central Park was also inspired by European parks such as Birkenhead Park near Liverpool in England. Unlike the Plaza de la Constitución and Boston Common, however, subsistence activities were banned in Central Park because it was designed as a landscaped natural space where New Yorkers could escape from urban problems and enjoy quiet recreation. This distinction resulted in Central Park being more commonly recognized as the first public park in the U.S.[9]

To better understand how public parks in the U.S. have emerged and why they failed to fulfill their democratic ideal as illustrated in the opening quotes of this chapter, it is worth reviewing the birth and evolution of Boston Common and Central Park more closely. Not only do these two parks hold a great deal of historical significance as the pioneering public parks in the U.S., but also their historical trajectories exhibit another set of interesting contradictions. Boston Common used to be a communal space owned and operated by all Bostonians, yet the elite gradually took away the people's authority.[10] In contrast, Central Park was built by White elites for the benefit of the middle- and upper-class White Americans; yet, once it was built, the working-class and immigrants repeatedly questioned the park's design and function to claim its governance.[11] In other words, Boston Common emerged with the city while Central Park was invented in the city. Interestingly, despite these differences between Boston Common and Central Park, they commonly share histories of greed, hypocrisy, prejudice, and ulterior motives of the rich and powerful.

European Colonialism, Aristocracy, and Boston Common

As was the case of the United States as a nation, what gave birth to Boston Common was European colonial invasion to the Americas. Many Indigenous tribes inhabited what is now called New England prior to European colonization. Due to its superior water supplies, Boston was named by the Massachusetts people as Shawmut, which roughly means "living fountains" in the Algonquin language.[12] Archaeological evidence and historical records indicate that Indigenous peoples fished, hunted, and farmed on Shawmut, including on the land of today's Boston Common, for at least millennia prior to European colonization.[13] However, European invaders, often misrepresented as "settlers," caused irrevocable disruption to Indigenous peoples' lives and their lands. In 1629, John Winthrop, the governor of the Massachusetts Bay Colony, declared that most land in America was "vacuum" because Indians had not "subdued" it, meaning that the land was there for the taking.[14] Indigenous peoples were gradually pushed out of the region through coercion, firearms, deceptive land treaties, and infectious diseases such as smallpox brought by European colonists—the displacement process began as early as the 1500s.[15]

During the 1600s, European colonists embarked on a number of American invasions and started to encroach on the Shawmut Peninsula. Reverend William Blaxton (also spelled Blackstone) was the first European who settled in Shawmut. He joined an expedition to America led by Robert Gorges which landed at Wessagusset (Weymouth, MA) in 1623. Although the expedition failed and most of the survivors returned to England, Blaxton wandered north and settled in the Shawmut Peninsula in 1625. He enjoyed a solitary life until the arrival of a group of English Puritans led by Governor John Winthrop in 1630. The Puritans first settled in Charles River, yet Blaxton invited them to Shawmut Peninsula for superior spring water. There, Winthrop's group started to build the governor's house and other residents, and it became the town of Trimountaine, later Boston. Yet, the Episcopalian Blaxton did not get along with the Puritans. In 1634, he decided to move to a less crowded area in Rhode Island and sold most of his 50-acre parcel of land to the Puritans for the purpose of using it as a common.[16]

According to Michael Rawson, early Bostonians used Boston Common as a multipurpose space. It had a graveyard and served as a place for cow grazing, festivals, elections, protests, executions, military training, and musters. Children played on the Common, and adults also enjoyed leisure walks and scenic views. Although they voted in 1646 to require new residents to rent or purchase the commonage right, a new vote in 1672 extended the right to all residents of the town. The Common affairs were addressed and managed through town meetings. Thus, access to the Common was a property right of Bostonians, and they were able to graze cows by paying a certain amount of tax. In this sense, the common was not really a public park since it was used for both subsistence and leisure. Rather, it was more of a public space for the everyday life of Bostonians.[17]

Despite the communal characteristic of the Common, historical research suggested that African Americans were not allowed to use it, not by the laws but by racist custom. This is not surprising given that the slavery system was firmly entrenched in the economic, political, and social landscape of Boston from its early days. The slave trade from Africa and the Caribbean began as early as 1638 in Boston, and from 1704 to 1752, the number of slaves in the town increased from 400 to 1,541, comprising nearly 10% of the town's population by the latter year, presumably an underestimation because slaves were taxable properties and slave owners often hid them from census trackers.[18] Negro Election Day (NED), also the General Election Day, was a special occasion on which Black Bostonians could use the Common, a principal holiday of Massachusetts when the General Court of Massachusetts chose its officers. NED was a popular event across New England towns, and it was a day that African Americans elected "Governors, Kings, and other officials" and held a festival consisting of parades, games, dinners, and dances.[19] In Boston, it is not clear if Black Bostonians elected officials on NED, but it was certainly a special annual festival where Black servants and apprentices were "allowed to have the unmolested use of the Boston Common, with an equality of rights and privileges with the white people." On other occasions, Blacks were not allowed to access the Common, and they were "hooted and driven from it with reproaches, insult, and force."[20]

The communal characteristics of Boston Common started to fade away during the late 1700s and the first half of the 1800s. The town experienced rapid economic expansion and its population almost doubled to 34,000 between 1790 and 1810. The class line became more explicit: Tax records show that from 1687 to 1770 the percentage of poor adult males who "perhaps rented a room, or slept in the back of a tavern, owned no property, doubled from 14 percent of the adult males to 29 percent." In 1771, the richest 10% in Boston had 57% of the wealth.[21] The wealthiest Bostonians began migrating to more rural areas such as Beacon Hill in order to emulate the European aristocracy, whose lifestyles included a large house with gardens and tree-lined streets. Moreover, in 1795, state officials' announcement of building a new State House on Beacon Hill triggered a building boom around the Common. Since living in a neighborhood near greenspace and civic buildings was considered a marker of gentility, by 1820, the neighborhood surrounding the Common became "an elite enclave" and by the early 1830s "more than a third of Boston's richest families lived on streets near the Common."[22]

Another critical incident that profoundly changed the character of Boston Common was Boston's transition from a town to a city in 1822. It entailed a shift from direct to representative democracy, meaning that Bostonians no longer cast their opinions through direct vote for city affairs, but instead elected public officials who could represent their interests.[23] Rawson notes that the political transition propelled the elitist bureaucracy: It quickly came to pass that a small group of wealthy individuals with political power controlled much of the city's affairs, imposing their upper-class sensibilities and environmental values on Boston Common. They started to restrict and ban working-class activities on the Common, such as cow grazing, carpet beating, gambling, and drinking. The goal was to elevate the cultural status and image of the Common by decoupling the space from any labors associated with the lower class and establishing a closer connection with a pastoral natural environment reminiscent of European aristocracy.[24]

The working-class fiercely fought back, especially over cow grazing. The City Council formed a special committee to study the issue, but it was merely a formality, since the committee was chaired by Mayor Harrison Gray Otis, who owned and lived on the properties across from the Common. Indeed, his son-in-law William Foster was the one who filed a petition to remove the cows. The committee concluded that removal of cows is necessary for the safety and recreation of Boston citizens, especially for children and women. Although hundreds of working-class petitioners claimed that cow grazing had been the "privilege" of Bostonians since 1634, the city proceeded to ban cows from the Common in 1830. Although Otis and the City Council gestured to find a middle ground with the petitioners by granting a right of pasturage on the Common's flats west of Charles Street, it was an unfenced land, so citizens with cows to graze had to hire a full-time cow keeper out of their own pockets. Rawson described that, "after removal of cows from Boston in 1830, the Common became the first public park in America devoted entirely to recreation."[25]

Thus, the birth of the first public park in America appears to be the Boston oligarchy's backyard improvement project, disguised as a city beautification project. Although the population growth, large immigration, and economic expansion during the 1800s made revamping of city infrastructure seemingly inescapable, the elite selfishly managed the process, took away political power from the people, and made themselves the main beneficiaries of the changes to the Common. For example, with the cows gone, Granary Burying Ground became a "private recreational area for the Park Street abutters. By day, their children played and picnicked on the grounds, and on warm evenings the residents held outdoor suppers and spread champagne and strawberries over the flat-topped tombs." Their desire to instill upper class gentility and refinement on the Common even led to the effort to change its name to Washington Park as well as renaming Frog Pond to Crescent Pond or Quincy Lake to make them sound more genteel. These efforts, however, did not materialize.[26]

The case of Boston Common raises some critical questions about the legitimacy of cultural sophistication and gentility that elite Bostonians tried to instill within the Common. Why should cultural refinement and gentility be prioritized over the tangible and practical benefits, such as cow grazing, for the majority of citizens? Whose idea of refinement and gentility prevailed? Moreover, the history of Boston Common makes us ponder the rightfulness of the representative democracy which took away political power from the ordinary citizens and buttressed elitist authoritarianism. After all, could ordinary Bostonians have kept the Common for their cow grazing and leisure if Boston had not adopted representative democracy in 1822? What would the Common look like if Boston found an alternative political system that did not subjugate the working-class and people with less means and political power? While we cannot reverse history to address these questions, Nathaniel Shurtleff, the author of one of the most detailed accounts of the history of Boston Common, indicated that the city's transition from direct democracy to representative democracy had "completely subjected the poor beasts [cows], as well as their owners, to the mercies of a new regime."[27]

Elitism, Displacement, Social Control, and Central Park

Twenty-four years after Boston Common became the first American public park, social conditions for creating the first urban landscaped park in the nation emerged in New York City. The city was previously a land inhabited by the Native Manhattan people; yet, in 1626, the Dutch West India Company purchased the land under dubious circumstances in which it is impossible to know the identity of the Indigenous people who sold the land or whether or not they fully understood the terms. From 1790 to 1860, New York City transformed into the center of U.S. cosmopolitanism, international trade, and immigration, and its population increased from 33,131 to 813,669. Inevitably, such an exponential growth put enormous pressure on the city's infrastructure and economic and social orders, resulting in poor housing and sanitary conditions, prevailing poverty, spread of disease, and staggering mortality and crime rates.[28] Amid this unsettling time, Andrew Jackson Downing emerged as the most prominent park advocate in the U.S. Downing is referred to as the father of American landscape architecture and his first book, published in 1841, *A Treatise on the Theory and Practice of Landscape Gardening, Adapted to North America*, placed him as a national authority on landscape design. Downing was "an ardent admirer of European public parks" and "one of the first to articulate a comprehensive vision for American urban parks."[29] In 1848, Downing started lobbying for a public park in New York City, asserting that parks can provide various health, social, and cultural benefits to the city.

Yet, the beginning of Central Park is more explicitly tied to a group of the wealthiest New Yorkers. Returning from their family trip to Europe, Robert Bowne Minturn, one of the richest merchants in New York, and his wife, Anna Mary Wendell Minturn, were fully convinced that New York City needed a large landscape park similar to those in European countries. They met with their elite social circles and proposed the Jones Wood, a site on the East River in Manhattan, to be the location of a new public park. Furthermore, the Minturn Circle proposed that the park should be funded through a general tax levied on the populace instead of using benefits assessment taxes limited to the nearby residents, because the park would benefit all residents of the city. The proposal quickly gained the support from other wealthy merchants, bankers, politicians, and landowners in the city.[30]

But why a public park? Given the urban problems that swept the city, other strategies such as affordable housing, improving public sanitation and sewage systems, creating a strong police force, and providing employment and poverty relief programs would seem far more effective than creating a large landscape open space. According to Rosenzweig and Blackmar, urban elites justified a park on three main grounds: Utilitarianism, cultural and moral improvement of the masses, and expression of social advancement. First, they argued that creating a large park would alleviate population density and promote public health. Parks, as reservoirs of nature, were seen as an antidote to urban problems as well as a medical technology. Second, advocates claimed that the park would foster harmonious social interaction between the rich and the poor so that the latter would learn civility and gentility from the former (interestingly, not the other way around). Finally, they asserted that the park would be an artistic expression of social and cultural advancement of the city and nation. For years, Americans were embarrassed to be looked down upon by intellectuals abroad, since the young country ostensibly lacked cultural identity and artistic and literary accomplishments comparable to its European counterparts. It was on these three grounds that the Minturn Circle rationalized a general public tax to build a park benefiting "the public."[31]

Yet, rich historical evidence indicates that the park advocates had more selfish motives. One of their primary concerns was economic gain through real estate development. Members of the Minturn Circle owned properties within or near Jones Wood, and they proposed using a general public tax for the park construction so they could avoid large assessment taxes. Other major landowners, such as the State Senator James Beekman and his friends, diligently supported the Jones Wood plan because they saw an opportunity for substantial financial gain. Similarly, when the Jones Wood plan was rejected by the city's Special Committee on Parks, major landowners of the Upper West Side lobbied for the parkland to be expanded and relocated to the land where Central Park stands today, because they hoped that the park construction would displace the residents and beautify the communities surrounding their properties, which would have resulted in an increase in their property values. Collectively, people who showed the most enthusiasm for a public park were wealthy land speculators in the city, while most working-class New Yorkers were indifferent to or against the park's construction. All things considered, the park leaders' idea to rely on general taxation to fund a public park was hypocritical, at best. It was also untimely because New York City's economy was in a downward trend.[32] If the rich truly desired to address the urban problems in the city and elevate the cultural and social status of ordinary citizens, why didn't they donate their own lands or money for the park construction?

Another major interest of the park advocates was to use the park as a means of social control. Immersed in the elitist social reform ideal and republican benevolence, they believed that people with money and power themselves had a moral obligation to aid the wellbeing of the less fortunate. Hence, their fundamental stance on social reform almost exclusively focused on the social and cultural education of the working-class and poor immigrants, as if they were the culprit of various urban problems. The elite seemed to believe that their own class and social legitimacy could be solidified by improving the cultural and social refinement of the two groups, resulting in less rebellious resistance or class conflict. Parks were an effective tool to accomplish their mission in a more gentle and friendly manner than authoritative reform programs or coercive police force.[33]

Finally, the park advocates wanted to create a safe recreation space for middle- and upper-class White families, especially women and young children, by demarcating racial and class boundaries. Although the John Wood plan was later discarded and the park was built in mid- and upper Manhattan, where Central Park stands today, the location was far from the working-class and immigrants, making their access to the park costly and time-consuming, even though the park was almost five times as large as all the existing parks and squares in the city combined.[34] The construction of Central Park also displaced the poor residents in the city. Most of the 1600 people who lived on the parkland were poor Irish and German immigrants and African Americans, and two-thirds of the adult residents were unskilled workers who had no power to influence the park's construction. The final eviction orders from the city to clear the land for Central Park came in October 1857, during the worst depression of New York in 20 years.[35]

The demolition of Seneca Village is a particularly troubling outcome of the park's construction. Established in the 1820s, after some African Americans began to buy land between 81st and 89th Streets and 7th and 8th Avenues, Seneca Village was one of the few areas in New York where Blacks were allowed to own property. Notably, Black citizens' property ownership was tied to their suffrage, because in 1821 the state of New York required Black men to own at least $250 in property and hold residency for at least three years to be able to vote. In 1845, there were nearly 350 Black households that paid property tax in New York, and of them, only 26% were eligible to vote. A quarter of those were Seneca Village landowners. Hence, for Black New Yorkers, property ownership in Seneca Village was about building their own Black community through political autonomy and economic prosperities. Furthermore, Black elites who owned lands in Seneca Village were prominent social justice advocates. Albro and Mary Joseph Lyons, Reverend Theodore S. Wright, and Charles B. Ray were agents of the Underground Railroad and helped thousands of enslaved fugitives escape to freedom. One speculation is that the village's basements served as hiding places for Blacks who escaped slavery and Wright and Ray envisioned using their Seneca Village properties as stops on the Underground Railroad. Yet, the construction of Central Park erased Seneca Village from the map. To make matters worse, displaced Black renters in the village could not find jobs in Central Park during the severest depression, because the park was built by an all-White and male workforce.[36]

At the end of the park's construction, people who gained the greatest profits were major and longtime landowners. For example, a wealthy Scottish land speculator Archibald Watt owned much of the northern end of the parkland. Watt acquired most of his land in the late 1820s and early 1830s for $16~$25 per lot and received $350~$380 per lot from the city. However, Watt complained about the nearly 2,000% profit that took less than 30 years, arguing that he had endured substantial carrying costs such as taxes and mortgage interests. As Rosenzweig and Blackmar point out, Watt's complaint was not about losing money, but rather about not making *more* money.[37]

For the ordinary New Yorkers, they had to give up their land due to the eminent domain. Many of them complained that their land values and relocation costs were not fairly assessed and they had to give up the land that they cultivated.[38] When estimating land values, city officials did not consider the anguish, frustration, insecurity, and perhaps hopelessness that the poor residents and Black property owners in Seneca Village had to endure. How long would it take for Black New Yorkers to rebuild a safe and thriving community like Seneca Village? Given the displacement and its negative aftereffect on next generations of Black New Yorkers, it is highly questionable if the eminent domain for building a public park was really justifiable.

Once Central Park opened to the public, it quickly became a popular recreation amenity among the upper-class, and a stage for their conspicuous consumption. Rosenzweig and Blackmar note that carriage drives during the late afternoon in the park became a fixed ritual for many elite New Yorkers. By 1863, nearly two-thirds of the park visitors arrived by carriage, yet fewer than 3% of the city's households maintained private carriages due to their high cost. At that time, the annual cost of operating a two-wheel tandem, which was touted for its affordability was about $1,500, while an average annual income for a member of the working-class, such as bakers, shoemakers, and the people who actually built the park, was approximately $300. The elites enjoyed showing off their material possession through carriages, horses, coachmen, and clothes. Working-class families constituted no more than 12.5% of the total annual visitors to the park, while they made up approximately 67% of the city's population. Most of them lived in lower Manhattan far away from the park, and the cost of a round trip using street railway was a substantial expenditure for them.[39]

While New York elites established "an unwritten set of social rules for who should use the park, for what purpose, and at what time," Olmsted and the park commission also ensured that Central Park was used in accordance with *their definition* of a public park—a vision that adheres to middle- and upper-class sensibilities.[40] Influenced by transcendentalist Ralph Waldo Emerson and landscape designer Andrew Jackson Downing, Olmsted defined Central Park as a carefully designed work of art that encapsulates a rustic natural environment in the middle of the highly urbanized city. As such, Olmsted believed park visitors should be "trained" to properly appreciate the natural aesthetic of Central Park and created a park police force that was informed by that of London's West End Parks, to enforce "fundamentally instructional" policing rules consistent with upper-class mores in the name of cultural development and refinement.[41] What followed next was *criminalization* of working-class leisure. Olmsted and other park commissioners only allowed quiet and individualistic recreation activities that promoted contemplative experience, prohibiting popular working-class recreation such as dancing, drinking, gambling, picnicking, and vigorous sport activities.[42]

Despite the baseball boom in the mid-1800s, Olmsted and park commissioners rejected all requests to play baseball in Central Park, arguing that the park could not accommodate large numbers of baseball players and spectators and that its refined natural beauty should be protected for the enjoyment of broader users. He also rejected the common council's offer to finance music concerts held on Saturday afternoons, so that he could maintain financial control and selectively choose the concert location and music genre.[43] By doing so, Olmsted and other park commissioners intended to create an atmosphere of tranquility and decorum that the working-class could emulate. But the timing of the concerts was not ideal for the working-class at all because they were still at work on Saturday afternoon. Because of the criminalization of working-class leisure, interaction between the working- and upper-class was often awkward and hostile, sometimes escalating into class conflicts, contradicting park leaders' claim of the park closing class gaps.[44]

By all accounts, the idea of creating Central Park was driven and actualized by the interests of the wealthiest and most powerful White individuals and social reformers in the city. They galvanized social and political power to build a large landscape public park, displaced the poor residents on the parkland, and worked diligently to imbue middle- and upper-class mores within the park.

Accordingly, the park was used disproportionally by White middle- and upper-class families, and the working-class and immigrants accounted for a small portion of park users. This series of historical events encompassing Central Park presents little to no resemblance to the park leaders' repeated emphasis on the democratic and inclusive character of the park. Did they really believe that they were creating a democratic public space, or had they confused "democracy" with their own biases about social order and practice? Perhaps more importantly, was their democratic assertion simply a disguise for their avarice and desire for social control? Although many generations of Americans have cherished Central Park as one of the most innovative urban planning projects in the history of the United States, it is also marked by displacement of the poor and powerless, gentrification, and reinforcement of class and racial boundaries—all the park injustice still occurring in America today.

After Central Park: Continuing Exclusion of the Poor and People of Color

The creation of Central Park poured gasoline on the spark of interest in public parks across the nation. The park earned a reputation as the most impressive architectural landscape work in the U.S. and was even admired in Europe. Many urban White elites in other major American cities were possessed by a fervent urge to build a similar landmark park in their communities. American urban parks and recreation movements emerged as a trend among wealthy and educated White men and women who espoused the paternalistic reform ideal that they were responsible for aiding the less fortunate.[45] Olmsted earned national notoriety and built many other landscape parks throughout the nation by replicating or slightly altering the Central Park model. His landscape work also extended to university campuses, cemeteries, playgrounds, residential subdivisions, and private estates.[46]

Naturally, Olmsted's definition of public parks and proper park behaviors was disseminated across the nation and set the tone for the design, funding mechanism, and managerial philosophy of the first generation of American community parks. Many park developments in other U.S. cities exhibited patterns of oppression and marginalization of the poor and people of color that were almost identical to the problems afoot in Boston Common and Central Park. Urban White elites and social reformers controlled much of park planning and development. They rationalized park construction via evangelical descriptions that public parks are elixirs for various urban problems and archetypes of social and cultural progress. They asserted that creating parks would improve public health conditions, beautify urban environments, bridge class lines through harmonious interaction, and provide wholesome recreation for everybody.[47]

Yet, the ways in which parks were built and managed indicate that those assertions were nothing but *empty rhetoric*. Park leaders preferred very specific demographics and park behaviors, built public parks away from racially mixed cities, and enforced strict park regulations to ensure visitor behaviors consistent with middle-class norms. Moreover, the leaders of parks and recreation movements viewed public parks and playgrounds as a means of social control and used parks and recreation programs to civilize the masses and Americanize immigrants.[48] They did so not because they were altruists or humanitarians, but because they believed that the cultural advancement and Americanization of immigrants would help legitimize the elite's social and cultural standing and would result in fewer assaults to their dominant social position and middle-class sensibilities. Their main target was children. They developed youth recreation programs to imbue American nationalism, militarism, and patriotism, believing that, for social reform purposes, teaching children is easier than teaching adults.[49]

Some officials were more blatant in their sinister intentions of using public parks. James H. Preston, the Mayor of Baltimore, presided over the city's first government-sponsored Black removal project. By the time Preston came to power in 1911, the neighborhoods around today's Mercy Medical Center and the city's courthouse were thriving multiracial communities anchored by an educational institution named after Frederick Douglass. The neighborhoods were also home to three powerful churches, including the nation's oldest Catholic Church catering to African Americans. It was a highly desired area for African Americans where they could enjoy full property rights. Yet, to stop the growth of the communities and prevent African Americans' encroachment to Mount Vernon and other high-class White neighborhoods, Preston copied a pioneering condemnation law he learned while visiting London and quickly acquired and demolished the courthouse neighborhoods. Moreover, he built a linear park stretching from Lexington Street and Centre Street to demarcate the racial boundaries within the city. He pioneered the deliberate use of condemnation as a tool of land-acquisition and racial segregation. In 1917, during the construction of the Preston Gardens Park, which was named after him, the mayor announced his plan for introducing a racial segregation ordinance in the city, stating that the mortality rates among African Americans for all forms of tuberculosis is 260.4% higher than among Whites. Preston denounced that African Americans "constitute a menace to the health of the White population."[50]

During the 20th century, moreover, cities throughout the South initiated a complex set of laws and planning practices to separate White and Black citizens. The city of Birmingham, Alabama hired Boston landscape designer Warren H. Manning and later the Olmsted Brothers, a landscape firm established by Frederick Olmsted's sons, for its comprehensive zoning project. Although both Manning and the Olmsted firm recommended a substantial increase in park and recreation space and the construction of a water-based park along Village Creek to control flooding, the city ignored the recommendation and zoned nearby areas of Village Creek for occupancy by African American households. By doing so, the city not only discarded a major park system, but also inflicted disproportional flooding risk on its African American citizens. Further, in 1910, the board of aldermen in the city adopted legislation denying Black citizens access to city-owned parks. No city-owned parks were available to African Americans until the construction of Memorial Park in the South Elyton neighborhood in 1942. In 1961, when the U.S. District Court judge H. H. Groom ruled that segregation of parks was unconstitutional and that they should be integrated by January 15, 1962, the Birmingham City Commission responded with an 80% cut of the park budget, forcing the Park and Recreation Board to close the parks and lay off 125 park employees effective on January 1st, 1962.[51]

Many people of color and White allies fiercely fought back to gain equal access to public parks. There were numerous protests, sit-ins, lawsuits, and formal and informal complaints against city and park officials. These efforts for justice were usually met with terrorism, violence, intimidation, and harassment from other White citizens and police officers. For example, during the Great Migration, White gangs routinely attacked African Americans who used public parks in the South Side area in Chicago—what used to be a collection of exclusively White spaces.[52] In 1946, when city officials in St. Louis, Missouri changed Buder Park from a White playground to an African American playground to accommodate the influx of African American families, the Ku Klux Klan burned a ten-foot tall cross and left behind a white hood with the letters "KKK" emblazoned across the brow.[53] On Memorial Day in 1961, an African American teenager at Griffith Park in Los Angeles was mercilessly beaten by police officers when he was accused of not paying for a merry-go-around ticket and refused to obey the police order. When the police started to beat other Black youths who intervened in the situation, it quickly escalated into a major race riot. Armed with bottles and rocks, Black youth repeatedly shouted, "This is not Alabama!" The police arrested several Black youths, blocked all park entrances, and closed the park temporarily.[54] During the 20th century, public parks throughout the nation frequently turned into intense battlegrounds for racial equality and justice.

Privatization and *park closures* were the most successful tactics White racists used to keep people of color out of public parks before and after the Civil Rights Act in 1964.[55] Public parks owned and managed by municipalities were obligated to follow desegregation orders due to their fundamental mission to serve the public, yet private operation offered a loophole. Municipalities across America either leased or sold their parks to private clubs to make the parks exempt from the Civil Rights Act or they simply closed the parks by citing potential racial conflict and violence as a threat to public safety. The city of Edwards, Mississippi formed a non-profit stock corporation to sell its recreational parks and swimming pools and operated them as private clubs restricted to invitational membership. When a class action on behalf of "all Negroes and poor persons residing in Edwards, Mississippi" was filed in a federal district court against the city, the motion for injunctive relief was denied and the complaint was dismissed.[56]

The above critical review of the history of community and urban parks in the U.S. illustrates that there has been little to no change in the historical patterns of park oppression and injustice. From Boston Common and Central Park to the community and urban public parks during the first half of the 20th century, many parks were founded upon elitism, classism, and racism of the White ruling class under the guise of inclusive democracy, good health, social improvement, and cultural advantages. The construction of new parks has been routinely glorified as social and cultural progress providing benefits to all citizens, yet the process was riddled with displacement, disenfranchisement, criminalization, and violence against the working-class and people of color. At the end, the White ruling class were the ones who gained the most benefits out of their park projects.

Enduring Park Injustice: Contemporary Examples

Sadly, the logic of park injustice lives on. Researchers have documented that today's communities of color and the poor suffer from inequitable park access largely due to the historical injustice and discrimination in public park provision.[57] A recent estimate shows that on average, communities of color have 44% less park acreage than majority White neighborhoods while low-income communities have 42% less park acreage than high-income neighborhoods.[58] Furthermore, inequitable park access is not limited to the quantity or availability of parks. Researchers have stressed that the quality of parks is another major issue, documenting that the public parks in neighborhoods of the working-class and people of color tend to be historically underfunded, crowded, poorly maintained, and crime-ridden.[59]

Statistically significant associations between the redlining practice in the 1930s and the contemporary park disparities provide powerful empirical evidence illustrating the enduring, diehard park injustice in the U.S. *Redlining* is a discriminatory housing policy established by the U.S. federal agencies during the 1930s which used color-coding to rank different areas of American cities based on the level of risk in real estate investment. The assessment of risk was arbitrary at best and heavily based on the racial composition of communities. It categorized most African American urban communities as Red or "Type D" neighborhoods, the riskiest areas for banks to make real estate investment and mortgage support, discouraging African American property ownership. While this redlining practice led to generational housing insecurity and unjust impoverishment of people of color, studies using various research methods consistently found that the neighborhoods previously categorized as Red or Type D now have significantly lower rates of greenspace and tree canopy as well as higher rates of the heat island effect compared to the Type A neighborhoods. Their findings indicate that today's park disparities across American cities are not random incidents: They are the consequence of centuries of deliberate and systematic oppression towards people with limited power and resources.[60]

Although many park officials, environmental organizations, and citizen groups are working hard to address inequitable park access and quality, people with power and privilege continue to control and take advantage of park developments in today's American society. For example, during the early stage of new park developments, affluent and powerful park boosters such as politicians, businessmen, and leaders of environmental and conservation organizations deploy a series of park rhetoric or "greensplaining," which consists of rosy descriptions about the park, highlighting its various benefits. Through this tactic, park leaders attain broader public, political, and media support for the park project. Meanwhile, the same rhetoric effectively muffles dissenting voices and conceals selfish motives, such as economic gain from real estate development, displacement of the poor, reinforcement of residential racial segregation, and/or creation of recreation infrastructure for rich White people.[61]

Park or green gentrification is a common byproduct of this logic of park oppression. Newly developed or renovated parks often result in a substantial increase in property values and sudden changes in community atmosphere. Subsequently, park development attracts wealthier and White migrants while exerting displacement pressure on poor local residents, through high property tax and feelings of being "out of the place." The irony, of course, is that they are supposedly the main beneficiaries of the park projects. Many U.S. cities have experienced this "green space paradox" which exacerbates the deprivation of park space from already disadvantaged and disfranchised local residents.[62] Consequently, park developments disproportionally benefit a group of park supporters who hold more privileges while devastating underprivileged people who were already marginalized—all too familiar stories.

Commercialization is another negative consequence of contemporary park developments. Due to the tightening of public tax support, government officials and park agencies are increasingly dependent on private funding for new park projects. While private-public partnerships have become a common practice in public park development in the U.S., the injection of private funding inevitably means the park location, design, and function are influenced, or worse, controlled by commercial interests rather than by the needs of local residents.[63] Through his investigation on the three post-industrial parks, the High Line in New York City, Bloomingdale Trail in

Chicago, and Buffalo Bayou Park in Houston, Kevin Loughran observed that privatization tainted the core identity of public parks as communal leisure space, redefining them as multifunctional space marked by consumption of coffees, wines, and artisanal foods. By normalizing consumptive activities within the parks, creeping privatization conjures a new form of social control and exclusion mechanism against the poor, people of color, the homeless, and people with disabilities—the people who do not align with bourgeois and consumerist norms of park use. Loughran concluded that "these parks are not really about nature, but about money and branding and prestige—and that even their 'nature' is more often about aesthetics than ecology."[64]

Hiding Behind the Shield of the Presumption

> ...like motherhood, parks symbolized something good, and therefore anyone who fought for parks fought under the shield of the presumption that he was fighting for the right—and anyone who opposed him, for wrong.
> From *The Power Broker*, a biography of Robert Moses written by Robert Caro[65]

Robert Moses, a controversial American park planner during the 20th century, and Frederick Law Olmsted were involved in more park development than any other individuals anywhere in the world. Moses created 15 major parks and 175 miles of parkways when he was the President of Long Island State Park Commission (1924–63) and also acquired 8,175 hectors of parkland and built 15 large swimming pools, 658 playgrounds, and 17 miles of public beaches as the Commissioner of the New York City Department of Parks (1934–60).[66] While Moses championed public parks provision in his era, Robert Caro notes that he was not only keenly aware of the widespread yet deceiving positive image surrounding public parks but also cunningly used it to create many public parks and extensive parkways in New York City.

Although some of Caro's claims on Moses have come under intense academic scrutiny, an indisputable fact seems to be that Moses was hardly the only one who hid behind "the shield of the presumption."[67] As illustrated in this chapter, an excruciatingly clear pattern cutting across the chronological reality of community and urban parks in the U.S. is the stark contrast between park leaders' utopian promises on what parks could provide to the people and the suffering that the people actually endured during and after parks were created. Many of the White ruling class have deviously used public parks as a tool to materialize their own interests at the expense of the lives and wellbeing of people with limited means and power.

As the history of community and urban parks, the first type of American public parks, is riddled with greed, hypocrisy, prejudice, and ulterior motives of the rich and the powerful, one might wonder how this disturbing pattern later evolved within the contexts of other public parks such as state and national parks. As illustrated in the next chapters, the truth is a hard one. In its urban infancy, the violence and oppression in American public parks had only just begun.

Notes

1 F. L. Olmsted, Letter to John Olmsted, January 14 1858 Fredrick Law Olmsted Papers, Library of Congress.
2 William Henry Chafe, Robert Korstad, and Raymond Gavins, *Remembering Jim Crow: African Americans Tell About Life in the Segregated South*, eds. William Henry Chafe, Raymond Gavins, and Robert Korstad (The New Press, 2001), 186.
3 For the biography of Olmsted, see Laura Wood Roper, *F.L.O: A biography of Frederick Law Olmsted* (Johns Hopkins University Press, 1973). Olmsted's park planning career and principle, see Dorceta E Taylor, "Central Park as a model for social control: urban parks, social class and leisure behavior in nineteenth-century America," *Journal of Leisure Research* 31, no. 4 (1999): 427–28. Dorceta E Taylor, *The Environment and the People in American Cities, 1600s–1900s: Disorder, Inequality, and Social Change* (Duke University Press, 2009), 260–62.
4 Andrew W. Kahrl and Malcolm Cammeron, *African American Outdoor Recreation* (U.S. Department of the Interior National Park Service, 2022); Victoria W. Wolcott, *Race, Riots, and Roller Coasters: The Struggle Over Segregated Recreation in America* (University of Pennsylvania Press, 2012); Myron F. Floyd and Rasul A. Mowatt, "Leisure among African Americans " in *Race, Ethnicity, and Leisure*, eds. Monika Stodolska et al. (Human Kinetics, 2013).
5 Carl D. Halbert, *Plaza de la Constitucion: The Archaeology of One of St. Augustine's Oldest Landmarks*, George A. Smathers Libraries, University of Florida (Gainesville, FL, 1996), https://ufdc.ufl.edu/UF00095508/00030.
6 John R. Stilgoe, "Town common and village green in New England: 1620–1981," in *On Common Ground: Caring for Shared Land from Town Common to Urban Park*, eds. Ronald Lee Fleming and Lauri A. Halderman (Harvard Common Press, 1982).
7 Michael Rawson, *Eden on the Charles: The Making of Boston* (Harvard University Press, 2010), 25.
8 For the enclosure of commons in England, see Christopher Dyer, "Conflict in the landscape: The enclosure movement in England, 1220–1349," *Landscape History* 28, no. 1 (2006): 21–33; Briony McDonagh, "Making and breaking property: Negotiating enclosure and common rights in sixteenth-century England," *History Workshop Journal* 76, no. 1 (2013): 32–56. For common lands in New England, see Stilgoe, "Town common and village green in New England."
9 Roy Rosenzweig and Elizabeth Blackmar, *The Park and the People: A History of Central Park* (Cornell University Press, 1998); Taylor, "Central Park as a model for social control."
10 Rawson, *Eden on the Charles*, Chapter 1.
11 Rosenzweig and Blackmar, *The Park and the People*; Taylor, "Central Park as a model for social control."
12 Rawson, *Eden on the Charles*, 11.
13 Joseph M. Bagley, "A prehistory of Boston Common," *Bulletin of the Massachusetts Archaeological Society* 68, no. 1 (2007); Massachusetts Historical Commission, *Historic and archaeological resources of the Boston area: A framework for preservation decisions*, Massachusetts Historical Commission (Boston, MA, 1982).
14 Francis Jennings, "Virgin land and savage people," *American Quarterly* 23, no. 4 (1971): 521.

15 Dunbar-Ortiz, *An Indigenous Peoples' History of the United States*; Roxanne Dunbar-Ortiz, *Not "a Nation of Immigrants": Settler Colonialism, White Supremacy, and a History of Erasure and Exclusion* (Beacon Press, 2021).
16 Walter Muir Whitehill, *Boston: A Topographical History* (The Belknap Press, 1968), 3–4; Nathaniel Bradstreet Shurtleff, *A Topographical and Historical Description of Boston* (Rockwell and Churchill, 1891), 24–26, Chapter 21.
17 Rawson, *Eden on the Charles*, Chapter 1.
18 Jared Ross Hardesty, *Unfreedom: Slavery and Dependence in Eighteenth-Century Boston* (New York University Press, 2018), 22.
19 Joseph Patrick Reidy, "'Negro Election Day' & Black Community Life in New England, 1750–1860," *Marxist Perspectives* (Fall 1978): 102; Shurtleff, Nathaniel Bradstreet, "May Meeting, 1873. Negro Election Day; I. H. to Dr. Sloane," *Proceedings of the Massachusetts Historical Society* 13 (1873).
20 Shurtleff, "May Meeting, 1873. Negro Election Day; I. H. to Dr. Sloane," 45, 46.
21 Rawson, *Eden on the Charles*, 32. For the tax record, Howard Zinn, *A People's History of the United States* (HarperCollins, 2015), 49; Gary B. Nash, *Class and Society in Early America* (Prentice Hall, 1970), 112.
22 Rawson, *Eden on the Charles*, 54, 34.
23 Shurtleff, *A Topographical and Historical Description of Boston*.
24 Rawson, *Eden on the Charles*.
25 Rawson, 58–64, 3.
26 For the quote, Rawson, 60. For the name change, Rawson, 67.
27 Shurtleff, *A Topographical and Historical Description of Boston*, 63–64.
28 For the land purchase, see Robert S. Grumet, *First Manhattans: A History of the Indians of Greater New York* (University of Oklahoma Press, 2012), 29. For the New York City, Edward L. Glaeser, "Urban colossus: Why is New York America's largest city?," 11, no. 2 (2005). For the urban problem, see Taylor, *The Environment and the People in American Cities*.
29 Taylor, "Central Park as a model for social control," 430.
30 Rosenzweig and Blackmar, *The Park and the People*, 16–18; Dorceta E. Taylor, "Equity, influence, and access: Central Park's role in historical and contemporary urban park financing," in *Environment and Social Justice: An International Perspective*, Research in Social Problems and Public Policy (2010).
31 Rosenzweig and Blackmar, *The Park and the People*, 23.
32 Rosenzweig and Blackmar, *The Park and the People*, Chapter 1 and 2; Taylor, "Equity, influence, and access," 34–36.
33 Taylor, "Central Park as a model for social control"; Taylor, *The Environment and the People in American Cities*, 287; Terence Young, "Social reform through parks: the American civic association's program for a better America," *Journal of Historical Geography* 22, no. 4 (1996).
34 "Imagining social justice and the false promise of urban park design," *Environment and Planning A: Economy and Space* 50, no. 2; Kevin Loughran, "Race and the construction of city and nature," *Environment and Planning A* 49, no. 9 (2017); Taylor, "Central Park as a model for social control."
35 Rosenzweig and Blackmar, *The Park and the People*, Chapter 3.
36 Sara Cedar Miller, *Before Central Park* (Columbia University Press, 2022), 176–78, 227; H. T. Gilligan, "An entire Manhattan village owned by black people was destroyed to build Central Park," *Timeline* (February 22, 2017). https://timeline.com/black-village-destroyed-central-park-6356723113fa. For the depression, Taylor, "Equity, influence, and access," 40.

37 Rosenzweig and Blackmar, *The Park and the People*, 85.
38 Ibid., 88, 91. Miller, *Before Central Park*, 306.
39 Rosenzweig and Blackmar, *The Park and the People*, 214, 32; Taylor, "Central Park as a model for social control," 459.
40 Rosenzweig and Blackmar, *The Park and the People*, 215.
41 David Schuyler, *The New Urban Landscape: The Redefinition of City Form in Nineteenth Century America* (Johns Hopkins University Press, 1986), 94; David Thacher, "Olmsted's Police," *Law and History Review* 33, no. 3 (2015): 606.
42 Geoffrey Blodgett, "Frederick Law Olmsted: Landscape architecture as conservative reform," *The Journal of American History* 62, no. 4 (1976); Catharine Ward Thompson, "Historic American parks and contemporary needs," *Landscape Journal* 17, no. 1 (1998).
43 Rosenzweig and Blackmar, *The Park and the People*, 249, 226.
44 Taylor, "Central Park as a model for social control," 428.
45 Daniel M. Bluestone, *Constructing Chicago* (Yale University Press, 1991); Alexander Garvin, *Public Parks: The Key to Livable Communities* (W. W. Norton & Company, 2011); Blodgett, "Frederick Law Olmsted."
46 Taylor, "Central Park as a model for social control," 434–35.
47 Taylor, 460–466; Galen Cranz, *The Politics of Park Design: A History of Urban Parks in America* (MIT Press, 1982); Galen Cranz and Michael Boland, "Defininig the sustainable park: A fifth model for urban parks," *Landscape Journal* 23, no. 2 (2004).
48 Benjamin Shepard and Gregory Smithsimon, *The Beach Beneath the Streets: Contesting New York City's Public Spaces* (SUNY Press, 2011). David Scott, "Race, ethnicity and leisure services practice: Can we hope to escape the past," in *Race, Ethnicity and Leisure*, eds. M. Shinew, K. J. Floyd, M. F. Walker, and G. J. Stodolska (Human Kinetics, 2014); Wayne Stormann, "The ideology of the American urban parks and recreation movement: Past and future," *Leisure Sciences* 13, no. 2 (1991).
49 Kenneth E. Mobily, "Immigration restriction, 'Americanization' and the Playground Movement," *Annals of Leisure Research* 24, no. 2 (2019); Taylor, "Central Park as a model for social control."; Young, "Social reform through parks."
50 Antero Pietila, *Not in My Neighborhood: How Bigotry Shaped a Great American City* (Rowman & Littlefield, 2010), 51, 52.
51 Charles E. Connerly, *"The Most Segregated City in America": City Planning and Civil Rights in Birmingham, 1920–1980* (University of Virginia Press, 2005), 36, 223, 180.
52 Brian McCammack, *Landscapes of Hope: Nature and the Great Migration in Chicago* (Harvard University Press, 2017), 30.
53 Joseph Heathcott, "Black archipelago: Politics and civic life in the Jim Crow city," *Journal of Social History* 38, no. 3 (2005): 726.
54 Josh Sides, *LA City Limits: African American Los Angeles from the Great Depression to the Present* (University of California Press, 2003), 173.
55 Wolcott, *Race, Riots, and Roller Coasters*.
56 Race Relation Law Reporter, "White, et al. v. City of Edwards, et al.," 11, no. 4 (1966): 1994.
57 Jason Byrne and Jennifer Wolch, "Nature, race, and parks: past research and future directions for geographic research," *Progress in Human Geography* 33,

no. 6 (2009), https://doi.org/10.1177/0309132509103156; Jason Byrne, Jennifer Wolch, and Jin Zhang, "Planning for environmental justice in an urban national park," *Journal of Environmental Planning and Management* 52, no. 3 (2009), https://doi.org/10.1080/09640560802703256; Alessandro Rigolon, "A complex landscape of inequity in access to urban parks: A literature review," *Landscape and Urban Planning* 153 (2016).

58 The Trust for Public Land, *The Heat Is On: A Trust for Public Land Special Report* (San Francisco, CA, 2020), https://www.tpl.org/wp-content/uploads/2020/09/The-Heat-is-on_A-Trust-for-Public-Land_special-report_r1_2.pdf.

59 Gavin Jenkins et al., "Disparities in Quality of Park Play Spaces between Two Cities with Diverse Income and Race/Ethnicity Composition: A Pilot Study," *International Journal of Environmental Research and Public Health* 12, no. 7 (2015); Alessandro Rigolon, Matthew Browning, and Viniece Jennings, "Inequities in the quality of urban park systems: An environmental justice investigation of cities in the United States," *Landscape and Urban Planning* 178 (2018); Chona Sister, Jennifer Wolch, and John Wilson, "Got green? Addressing environmental justice in park provision," *GeoJournal* 75, no. 3 (2010); Monika Stodolska et al., "Perceptions of urban parks as havens and contested terrains by Mexican-Americans in Chicago neighborhoods," *Leisure Sciences* 33, no. 2 (2011); Jennifer Wolch, John P. Wilson, and Jed Fehrenbach, "Parks and park funding in Los Angeles: An equity-mapping analysis," *Urban geography* 26, no. 1 (2005).

60 For the redlining, see Richard Rothstein, *The Color of Law: A Forgotten History of How Our Government Segregated America* (Liveright Publishing, 2017). For the redlining and greenspace, see Dexter H. Locke et al., "Residential housing segregation and urban tree canopy in 37 US Cities," *npj Urban Sustainability* 1, no. 1 (2021); Anthony Nardone et al., "Redlines and Greenspace: The Relationship between Historical Redlining and 2010 Greenspace across the United States," *Environmental Health Perspectives* 129, no. 1 (2021); David J. Nowak, Alexis Ellis, and Eric J. Greenfield, "The disparity in tree cover and ecosystem service values among redlining classes in the United States," *Landscape and Urban Planning* 221 (2022).

61 Kevin Loughran, *Parks for Profit: Selling Nature in the City* (Columbia University Press, 2022); Lauren E. Mullenbach, "Critical discourse analysis of urban park and public space development," *Cities* 120 (2022); Alessandro Rigolon et al., "'A park is not just a park': Toward counter-narratives to advance equitable green space policy in the United States," *Cities* 128 (2022); Lauren E. Mullenbach, Andrew J. Mowen, and Kathryn J. Brasier, "Urban parks, the growth machine, and the media: An analysis of press coverage of the high line, klyde warren park, and the rail park," *Environmental Sociology* (2021). For the term greensplaining, see Mariela Fernandez, Brandon Harris, and Jeff Rose, "Greensplaining environmental justice: A narrative of race, ethnicity, and justice in urban greenspace development," *Journal of Race, Ethnicity and the City* 2, no. 2 (2021).

62 Kenneth Gould and Tammy Lewis, *Green Gentrification: Urban Sustainability and the Struggle for Environmental Justice* (Routledge, 2016); Hamil Pearsall and Jillian K. Eller, "Locating the green space paradox: A study of gentrification and public green space accessibility in Philadelphia, Pennsylvania," *Landscape and Urban Planning* 195 (2020); Alessandro Rigolon and Jeremy Németh, "Toward a socioecological model of gentrification: How people, place, and policy shape neighborhood change," *Journal of Urban Affairs* 41, no. 7 (2019); Jennifer

R. Wolch, Jason Byrne, and Joshua P. Newell, "Urban green space, public health, and environmental justice: The challenge of making cities 'just green enough,'" *Landscape and Urban Planning* 125 (2014).
63 Taylor, "Equity, influence, and access."
64 Loughran, *Parks for Profit*, 136.
65 Robert A. Caro, *The Power Broker: Robert Moses and the Fall of New York* (Alfred A. Knopf, Inc, 1974), 193.
66 Garvin, *Public Parks*, 57.
67 For critiques on Caro, see Bernward Joerges, "Do politics have artefacts?" *Social Studies of Science* 29, no. 3 (1999); Steve Woolgar and Geoff Cooper, "Do artefacts have ambivalence: Moses' bridges, winner's bridges and other urban legends in S&TS," *Social Studies of Science* 29, no. 3 (1999).

2 State Parks

For every person in South Carolina—the young, the old, the rich, the poor, the sportsman, the mother of a family, the laborer, the farmer, the college professor, and all others—there is a State park within approximately fifty miles of home, where picnic shelters provide for a day's outing, where sanitary bathing facilities may be found, or well equipped cabins accommodate guests for a longer vacation.

A guide of South Carolina State Parks in 1940[1]

I am inquiring of you if any provision has been made for the participation of Negroes in the use of Federal parks for camping, picnicking, hunting, and fishing in the State of Tennessee. For example, we are aware that several thousand acres of land are being developed by the National Park Service in cooperation with the State of Tennessee near Dixon, Tennessee. Under the present setup, will it be possible for our churches and Sunday Schools to visit the Montgomery - Bell Park for picnic and camping purposes, or for our youth work organization to hold a week's Summer Camp for groups of boys and girls respectively?

The letter from W. J. Faulkner of the Inter-Denominational Ministerial Alliance to Sam Brewster of the Department of Conservation of the State of Tennessee on August 26, 1937[2]

The 1940 guide of South Carolina State Parks emphasized that, regardless of class, gender, or occupational status, the parks were readily accessible and could provide quality leisure time to all South Carolinians. These descriptions perfectly mirror the ideal characteristics of state parks that the nation's park leaders proclaimed at the early stage of the state park movement during the 1920s. In fact, when the National Conference of State Parks emerged in the 1920s, its core mission was promoting democratic access to state parks for wholesome recreation.[3]

In this context, Faulkner's letter is rather puzzling. The president of Nashville's Inter-Denominational Ministerial Alliance, an African American clergy organization, inquired of Tennessee's Department of Conservation whether African American citizens would be able to use

DOI: 10.4324/9781032707624-4

the newly developed Montgomery Bell Recreational Demonstration Area. Recreational Demonstration Areas (RDAs) were public parks developed by the National Park Service through the labor and funding provided by federal relief programs, such as the Civilian Conservation Corps and the Works Progress Administration. As most RDAs were later turned into state parks, Montgomery Bell RDA also became Montgomery Bell State Park in 1943.[4]

Why would Faulkner need assurance of equal access if state parks were built with a mission to provide democratic access and quality recreation to all American citizens? A short answer is that there was a glaring disparity between the egalitarian vision of state park leaders and what was actually happening on the ground. This chapter uncovers this distinctive dissonance by tracing the beginning of state parks in the United States and how they have been built across the nation. Today, there are more than 9,800 state park units across the U.S., attracting more than 850 million people each year and serving as crucial health, conservation, and tourism infrastructure. However, similar to community and urban parks described in the previous chapter, the birth and expansion of state parks are rooted in avarice and nefarious intent. They are yet another example of Americans killing, displacing, excluding, and exploiting vulnerable and marginalized people.

The First State Parks

The early history of state parks in the U.S. is complex and multifaceted, and identifying the first state park is a contentious task. Yosemite is widely known as the first state park because the Yosemite Valley Act in 1864 designated the valley and nearby Mariposa Big Tree Grove as public lands and the federal government granted them to the state of California for "public use, resort, and recreation." Thus, until it became a national park in 1890, Yosemite was placed under the state administration and functioned as a state park for 26 years.[5] However, if we define state parks as state-owned public lands set aside for the purpose of recreation and nature conservation, historical records indicate that Yosemite might not be the first state park. Instead, the Indian Springs Reserve in central Georgia, which is currently Indian Springs State Park, established by a bill passed in 1827, is considered the oldest state park.[6] Interestingly, neither bill used the term "state park" or even "park" to define Indian Springs Reserve, Yosemite Valley, or Mariposa Big Tree Grove, even though they were, in a practical sense, used as state parks. According to Ney Landrum, a state park in northern Wisconsin created by the legislature in 1878 might be the first place of statutory use of the term "state park."[7]

Settler Colonialism and Ethnic Cleansing Against Indigenous Peoples

Whether it's Yosemite, Mariposa, or Indian Springs, we must understand that all of the earliest state parks in the U.S., or any parks for that matter, were established on the lands that European colonists robbed from

Indigenous peoples. It means that the history of American public parks is deeply intertwined with the history of the United States of America, a nation established through colonial conquest, ethnocide, slavery, and economic subjugation committed by Europeans and Americans against Indigenous peoples.[8]

Importantly, the beginning of these two histories can be traced back to one specific event, the arrival of Christopher Columbus in the Americas in 1492. James Loewen and Howard Zinn point out that most American history books are riddled with fabrications and omissions that make Christopher Columbus a hero, rendering many Americans ignorant of the astonishing scale of crimes that he and the Spaniards committed in the Americas. Throughout his four invasions (what most American history books erroneously describe as expeditions or journeys) to the Americas, Columbus had only one thing on his mind: plundering gold and anything valuable from the land.[9]

Columbus' method was barbarism: murder, enslavement, rape, and torture of Indigenous peoples. He and the Spaniards killed Indigenous peoples for sport and dog food, hanged or burned them to death, enslaved them and sold them in Spain, cut off their hands if they did not collect gold, and raped native women as young as nine years old. Indigenous peoples escaped or fought back with sticks and stones, yet such resistance had an unintended effect: It gave the plunderers a perfect excuse for war. Many Indigenous peoples committed mass suicide rather than endure the cruelty of the invaders. Moreover, the diseases brought by Europeans such as swine flu and smallpox significantly depopulated the Indigenous population.[10] Bartolomé de La Casas, a young priest who joined the conquest of Cuba, documented the horrifying scale of genocide committed by Columbus and the Spaniards. When he arrived on Hispaniola in 1508, La Casas wrote,

> There were 60,000 people living on this island, including the Indians; so that from 1494 to 1508, over three million people had perished from war, slavery, and the mines. Who in future generations will believe this? I myself writing it as a knowledgeable eyewitness can hardly believe it, but it is a fact born of our sins, and it will be well that in time to come we lament it.[11]

Sadly, Columbus' colonial conquests and barbaric crimes against Indigenous peoples set a clear model for later generations of Europeans and Euro-Americans—a model that echoes down through the history of the United States of America and the birth of its public parks. England, France, and the Netherlands soon joined the colonial invasion of the American continent. From the First Anglo-Powhatan War in Jamestown in 1609 to the Battle of Bear Valley in 1918, the history of the United States is punctuated by numerous wars and massacres against Indigenous peoples. Once the United States of America was established through the American Revolutionary War, the U.S. government enacted a number of legislations, such as the

Civilization Fund Act of 1819 and the Indian Removal Act of 1830, to wipe out Indigenous culture and forcibly displace them to Indian reservations.[12]

When public parks began to emerge during the 19th century, Americans' encroachments on Indigenous territories in the West once again resulted in many wars and massacres. These include the Dakota War in 1862, Snake War in 1864–68, Colorado War in 1864–65, Texas-Indian War from 1820–75, Great Sioux War in 187–77, and Wounded Knee Massacre in 1890, to name a few. Accordingly, the U.S. Army built at least six dozen military forts west of the Mississippi, and almost all of them were used to support campaigns against Indigenous peoples and the Westward expansion.[13]

Notably, though, Indigenous peoples lost more land by signing fraudulent and manipulative treaties than by warfare.[14] From the Revolutionary War to the turn of the 20th century, approximately 600 treaties were signed across the nation, resulting in nearly two million square miles of land being transferred from Indigenous peoples to the U.S. government.[15] More Indian treaties were "broken" by judges and justices who bent the law to achieve certain political ends than were ever broken by boomers and sooners. According to Deloria and DeMallie, "almost every president of the United States has promised, at some time during his term, that he would uphold the Indian treaties, and none has fulfilled the promise when decisions had to be made."[16]

Thus, what buttresses the inception of the United States of America as a nation is this ethos of colonial conquest, ethnic cleansing, and European and American imperialism.[17] As detailed in the rest of this chapter, this pattern of annihilation bears distinctive parallels with the ways in which some of the earliest and most iconic public parks in the U.S. were founded.[18]

Indian Removal, Hatred Treaty, and Indian Springs State Park

Even though Indian Springs State Park and Yosemite National Park are thousands of miles apart, their inceptions are commonly marked by European and American colonial conquests of Indigenous lands, displacement of Indigenous peoples, and bloodshed between the conquerors and the conquered. Indian Springs was a sacred place among Creek peoples before European and American colonists invaded their lands. The Creeks believed that the spring water possessed healing power and frequently visited the site to drink the water and cure sickness.[19] The Creek peoples consisted of many different Indigenous groups, and by the early 18th century, they had established towns across Georgia and Eastern Alabama and formed a powerful confederacy.[20] In 1792, Douglas Watson, a government scout, encountered the springs while running away from the Creeks, but soon fled the area because he sensed a strong gunpowder smell, fearing live firearms. A month later, Gabriel Dunlap, a hunter, accidentally stumbled upon the springs while also escaping from a band of Indigenous people. These two are known as the first White men who discovered the springs.[21]

In 1800, Chief William McIntosh, Tustunugee Hutkee, built a cabin at the springs and used it as a winter home for his family. Previously, the Creeks did not establish a residence there, because they believed that the noise of children and women would drive the healing power from the springs. After McIntosh broke this superstition, both Creek peoples and Whites started to establish habitations and enjoyed the springs rather peacefully for years. McIntosh realized the potential value of Indian Springs and built an inn in 1823 with his cousin, Joel Bailey. The inn contained 34 rooms, a dining room with a piano, and elaborate etchings on the walls. Many travelers visited his property to enjoy civilization in the wilderness, often on their way to New Orleans.[22]

Chief McIntosh is the main figure in the early history of Indian Springs. He was born of Captain William McIntosh of the British Army and a Creek woman in 1778 and was the first cousin to George M. Troup, who became Governor of Georgia in 1823. Troup's mother was Catharine McIntosh, a sister of Chief McIntosh's father. Because of this family background, McIntosh spoke English and held both American and Creek identities. Yet, historical records indicate that McIntosh was more closely affiliated with Americans: He encouraged the Creeks to adopt Western civilization and customs such as a centralized government system, cotton agriculture, owning slaves and lands, English-style education, and patrilineal descent. McIntosh himself possessed two plantations (Acorn Town and Indian Springs), grew cotton, and owned more than 100 slaves.[23]

Moreover, McIntosh strategically and cunningly used his dual identity to gain profit and recognition from both Americans and the Creeks. Since McIntosh spoke English and was accustomed to Southern American culture, Americans viewed him as a "civilized Indian" whom they could trust when dealing with Indian affairs. On several occasions, McIntosh helped orchestrate land treaties between Americans and Indigenous groups and in return received cash, annuities (cash and goods), and their distribution rights within Indigenous communities. For example, at the first Treaty of Indian Springs in 1821, McIntosh arranged for special land cessions for himself and obtained 1,000 acres of land at Indian Springs, 640 acres of land around his plantation on the west bank of the Ocmulgee River, and a cash reward of $40,000. During the War of 1812 and the First Seminole War in 1817, he even allied with General Andrew Jackson and rose from a Major to a Brigadier General in the U.S. Army. Creek peoples viewed McIntosh as a traitor, yet U.S. officials helped McIntosh establish his notoriety within the Creek Nation not only by frequently choosing him as a main distributor of bribes to the Creeks for land cessions, but also by making treaties with him even though he never represented the majority of Creeks. Because of his ability to secure cash and goods from the U.S. government and distribute them among Indigenous peoples, McIntosh emerged as a powerful leader of the Lower Creeks.[24]

As Americans continued their colonial invasions and pushed Indigenous peoples westward during the 18th and 19th centuries, McIntosh saw a slim chance that the Creeks may keep their homelands. In 1824, McIntosh and his Creek friends conspired for a major land treaty with U.S. treaty commissioners Duncan G. Campbell and James Meriwether, and possibly Georgia Governor Troup, to cede the land of the Creek Nation to the U.S. McIntosh requested the treaty would be signed in his own house and further demanded presidential protection, because he previously signed the laws of the Creek Nation that any chief signing a treaty of any land cession to Whites would be executed. To secure McIntosh's participation, the commissioners bribed him with a total of $40,000.[25]

When 400 Creek representatives and warriors arrived at Indian Springs to discuss the terms of the treaty, they were openly hostile and rejected the possibility of giving up more lands in Georgia. Opothle Yoholo, a representative of Big Warrior of the Upper Creeks, denounced the arrangement and gave a death warning to McIntosh not to sign the treaty. However, when most representatives left the meeting, McIntosh, the other 51 chiefs, and the U.S. officials signed the treaty anyway. Out of those 52 chiefs, only six were headmen and only McIntosh was a member of the Creek National Council. This controversial Treaty of Indian Springs in 1825 stipulated that the Creek Nation would cede all their lands in Georgia to the U.S. government in exchange for an equal amount of land west of the Mississippi along the Arkansas River, as well as $400,000 to compensate for abandoned improvements and transportation cost. Article 5 of the treaty, which the conspirators tried to hide, authorizes Campbell and Meriwether to control $200,000 of those $400,000 to be paid immediately to McIntosh and his friends.[26]

Opothle Yoholo was infuriated. He leaped upon a large rock that stood outside McIntosh's home and made a fiery speech that McIntosh's blood "shall wash out the memory of this hated treaty." A few months later, more than a hundred Creek warriors surrounded McIntosh's house in Chattahoochee and waited for a moment of revenge. Around three o'clock in the morning, the group began the execution of the traitor and set fire to his house. McIntosh fought back but was soon overwhelmed by the attacks. It is said that his body was penetrated by more than a hundred bullets, his tongue was cut out, and his scalp was taken to a Creek village. Samuel Hawkins, one of McIntosh's sons-in-law who lived nearby, was also killed.[27] McIntosh sold the Creek Nation on multiple occasions and his continuing betrayals eventually cost him his life.

Although the Treaty of Indian Springs in 1825 was signed, the Creeks did not move from Georgia. Instead, they protested its illegitimacy to the U.S. government and demanded justice. President John Quincy Adams recognized the unlawfulness of the treaty. He banned any further American encroachment into the Creek Nation and worked to rectify the situation. The Creek representatives visited Washington, D.C. to discuss resolutions, and eventually they signed the Treaty of Washington in 1826. This time, the Creeks agreed to cede their Georgia landholdings in exchange for a one-time payment of $217,600, an annual perpetuity of $20,000, and various material and labor support for the Creeks' relocation to lands west of the Mississippi River. The Washington Treaty also voided the previous treaty that was orchestrated by McIntosh and the others.[28]

It is against this backdrop of avarice, sinister plotting, bloodshed, and Indian removal that the first state park in the U.S., Indian Spring Reserve, came to be. After the Washington Treaty, the Georgia legislature passed an act in December 1827 making the ten acres centered by the spring into a public park. In 1927, the state officially renamed the site Indian Spring State Park.[29] Today, the Inn that McIntosh and Bailey built is still in operation as the Indian Spring Hotel/Museum. McIntosh is gone. But the desk on which the Treaty of Indian Springs was signed in 1825 still stands in the museum.

Wars, Capitalism, Economic Subjugation, and Yosemite

Much like Indian Springs, the early history of Yosemite is punctuated by White colonial invasion against Indigenous peoples. Indeed, Americans seized Yosemite Valley through warfare against Yosemite peoples, namely the Mariposa Indian War in 1850. Archeological evidence suggests human occupancy of the Yosemite area from B.C. 1000 or 2000, and by the time Americans penetrated the area for mining, fur trade, commercial hunting, and settlement, Yosemite Valley was home to the Ahwahneechee, a subgroup of the Southern Sierra Miwok.[30] The first American who spotted Yosemite Valley is still a subject of scholarly debate. Some claim that mountain man Joseph Walker saw the Valley while he led Benjamin Bonneville's fur trapping enterprise in 1833, yet the story has been challenged by a more rigorous historical reconstruction of the recorded travel route.[31] A more widely accepted story is that William P. Abrams and U.N. Reamer, both of whom worked at James D. Savage's trading post, accidentally encountered the amazing vista containing three of Yosemite's treasures—Bridalveil Fall, El Capitan, and Half Dome—while they were lost during a hunting excursion.[32]

James D. Savage, one of many forty-niners who moved to California in search of gold, is a central figure in the Mariposa Indian War. He had extensive knowledge of Indigenous languages and culture, established several trading posts in the area, and hired (or exploited) many of the Southern Sierra Miwok and Yokut peoples in his mining operations, marrying several of their women. Because of his influence, the Yosemite Indians called him "Blond King," and he also preferred to be called "El Rey Tulareños," meaning "King of the Tulares."[33]

Despite his prominence, Indigenous peoples developed animosity toward Savage because he frequently broke his promises and exploited Indigenous labor for gold mining. In the spring of 1850, Savage heard from his wives that the Yosemite Indians were plotting to drive the Whites out of the region. Later, he discovered that his trading post in Fresno was raided and three clerks were killed. Local Indigenous peoples were determined, and their resistance to the continuing deprivation of their rights, dispossession of their land, and exploitation of their labor escalated into more intense raids across the region. Governor John McDougal, who at one time spoke to the state legislature about the inevitability of the extermination of the Indians, authorized the formation of a local militia. The Mariposa Battalion, composed of 200 mountain men, was formed in 1851, and the governor commissioned Savage major of the battalion. Concerned with the Indian and settler conflicts, three U.S. Indian commissioners went to California from Washington, D.C. to prevent further bloodshed. They signed an agreement with several Indigenous groups specifying that they live on designated reservations. Yet others, including the Ahwahneechee in Yosemite Valley, refused to give up their homeland. In response, the state legislature authorized the governor to proceed with local action.[34]

Savage wanted revenge. His two companies left for the head of the Merced River to subdue the Yosemite and Nutchu and established headquarters that were likely near Alder Creek or Bishop Creek above the South Fork. Savage sent a messenger to Chief Tenaya of the Ahwahneechees and demanded a peaceful surrender and relocation of the group to an Indian reservation on the Fresno River. Tenaya himself came to the camp and acknowledged that his people preferred to stay in the valley. Since no agreement was reached between the two parties, Savage continued his march, spotted a portion of the Yosemite Valley along the way, probably near Old Observation Point, and eventually descended to the valley floor in March 1851. The battalion surgeon, Dr. Lafayette Houghton Bunnell, was deeply moved by the grandeur of the scene and suggested that the valley be called "Yosemity" after its native inhabitants. Savage and his army realized that the Ahwahneechee had already fled the scene and only one elderly woman who could not climb the mountains was left behind. Hence, Chief Tenaya probably pretended to negotiate with Savage to buy more time for the escape. Savage's army burned the dwellings and large caches of acorns, hoping to starve out the Yosemite from the Valley to reservations. Yet, Tenaya's band circled back to the battalion's camp near Mariposa.[35]

The second military operation led by Captain John Boling in May 1851 finally hunted down the Yosemite. In the process, Tenaya's three sons were shot and killed and all Indigenous captives were assigned to the Fresno River reservation. Tenaya, however, successfully petitioned to return to Yosemite Valley and other Indians also joined him later.[36] The battalion was mustered out of service in July 1851. Yet in May 1852, a conflict between the Yosemite and Americans broke out again, resulting in the death of two White miners and possibly an Indigenous child. Subsequently, a detachment of regular army troops under the command of Lieutenant Tredwell Moore was dispatched from Fort Miller to the valley, where they shot five Natives who had the White men's clothing, concluding the Mariposa Indian War.[37]

What followed the military invasion of Yosemite Valley was a capitalist invasion—an equally violent assault—in the form of tourism and commercial development. As early as 1855, White migrants started to build infrastructure and hotels to serve tourists. In 1855, an English businessman James Mason Hutchings learned about the majestic beauty of Yosemite and organized the first tourist party to the valley. Thoroughly moved by its grandeur and panoramic view, Hutchings and his party produced several writings and illustrations promoting the valley. Horace Greeley, the editor and publisher of the *New York Tribune*, and Thomas Starr King, a well-regarded Unitarian minister, lecturer, and author, also visited Yosemite and confirmed its exceptional natural wonder. C. L. Weed made the first photographs of the valley for Hutchings in 1859. The artist Albert Bierstadt visited the valley and produced several paintings.[38] Yosemite gained national and international reputations and became an icon of American culture and natural beauty. Consequently, the number of tourists to Yosemite increased rapidly. There were only 406 visitors to Yosemite Valley from 1855 to 1863; yet in 1864, the year that the Yosemite Park Act was signed, the Valley received 147 visitors and the number doubled the following year, reaching more than 1,100 with the completion of the transcontinental railroad in 1869.[39]

Alarmed by rapid tourism development in Yosemite and the loss of giant sequoia trees to lumber interests, Israel Ward Raymond, the California state representative of the Central American Steamship Transit Company of New York, wrote a letter to John Conness, the junior senator from California, and urged the preservation of Yosemite Valley and the Mariposa Grove of giant sequoias. In his letter written on February 20, 1864, Raymond underscored Yosemite's scenic appeal of national significance and argued that it should be "granted for public use, resort, and recreation," and "inalienable forever."[40] Raymond also included a photograph of the Yosemite landscape rendered by pioneering photographer Carlton Watkins to illustrate its sublime nature.[41]

But why was Israel Raymond, an executive of a steamship company, so concerned with environmental destruction in Yosemite, so much so that he was motivated to persuade a state senator to protect it? Raymond's desire to protect Yosemite was deeply intertwined with commercial interests, because his company was operating 23 steamships traveling between east coast ports and San Francisco. Therefore, federal protection of Yosemite would ensure increased and stable traffic in steamship lines and bring him more profits.[42] Moreover, Raymond was not alone in his rapacity. Senator Conness was well aware of Yosemite's potential to attract tourists to California and the fact that roadbuilding and railroad companies would strongly support the legislation.[43] Fredrick Law Olmsted, the co-designer and first superintendent of Central Park in New York City, also believed that Yosemite would serve as a major tourism destination of California, similar to the natural scenery of Switzerland. Olmsted was already gaining a national reputation, and Raymond listed him in the letter as one of the recommended commissioners of the Valley and Grove.[44] The two could have met each other either in New York or California, since Olmsted visited California in 1863 to manage the Mariposa Estate.[45] Thus, the Yosemite park supporters were not anti-development, nature preservationists. Rather, they were people very much interested in the financial benefits of tourism development and public recreation.[46] Commercial interests and nature preservation were inextricably entwined in the development of state and national parks.

Senator Conness forwarded Raymond's letter to the commissioner of the General Land Office and requested the preparation of a bill, which was soon accepted favorably by the Senate Committee on Public Lands on May 17, 1864. In his speech, Conness argued the importance of protecting public land from commercial development for recreation. He forcefully reminded the Senate of the fact that when America sent a cross-section of a giant sequoia tree to the World's Fair held in London, the British believed that it was a fabrication. He also noted that the purpose of the bill "is to make a grant to the State" which indicated that the federal government would hold no financial obligation for managing the lands, an appealing option for the federal government, since enormous expenses were already incurred during the height of the Civil War. Conness's bill calling on American patriotism was a success. The House of Representatives ratified the measure, and on June 30, 1864, President Abraham Lincoln signed the Yosemite Park Act into law. On April 2, 1866, the California legislature officially accepted the grant, making it the first state park in the nation given by the federal government.[47]

Although the American invasion and the creation of Yosemite Valley as a public park profoundly disrupted the lives of the Yosemite, they were also resilient. As the commercial development progressed in the Valley, the Yosemite adopted tourism as a new subsistence activity and cleverly took advantage of White tourists' naïve fascination with Indigenous culture. Using their knowledge of local geography, climate, and game animals, the Yosemite served as guides, charged fees for song and traditional dancing, provided fish and game, and sold their traditional baskets. Women worked as maids or laundresses in hotels and the homes of concessionaires. Due to the geographical remoteness, the Yosemite became an integral part of local tourism, which provided a means for them to remain in their home and earn a livelihood within the new capitalist economic system.[48]

Yet, history once again proved that it is difficult to survive through a wave of colonial and capitalist invasion. In the late 1880s, a large group of Indigenous leaders filed a petition to the U.S. president and Congress requesting $1 million compensation for "the destruction of every means of support for ourselves and families by the rapacious acts of the whites."[49] Although the petition was not advanced at the state hearing and no answer was provided by Washington, it was a clear sign of the widespread environmental destruction that had decimated Yosemite's high country. Indeed, tens of thousands of acres of prime timberland fell to lumbering and mining companies between 1881 and 1890. In 1890, environmentalists such as John Muir and Robert Underwood Johnson successfully petitioned the federal government's takeover of the park management, making Yosemite the third national park in the U.S.[50]

For the Indigenous peoples in Yosemite, the transition from state to national park did not make their life any easier. Newly arrived U.S. Cavalry banned any hunting activities within the park boundary. Moreover, park officials actively exploited the Indigenous culture to attract more tourists to the park. The Indian Field Days, an event consisting of various showcases of the native culture, was originally initiated by a park concessionaire Desmond Park Company in 1916.[51] Supposedly an event to revive and preserve the Indigenous culture, the park officials mainly cared for its effectiveness in enticing tourists and encouraged the Yosemite to conform to "a generic representation of Great Plains culture."[52] For the most part, the Field Days was not an important event for the Yosemite, even though they participated and derived certain benefits.[53]

The Yosemite had been able to stay in the Village because their labor and presence were important for tourism, yet this unique and more or less peaceful circumstance started to deteriorate during the late 1920s. Superintendent Washington Lewis wanted to move the Yosemite residents to another location within the Valley in order to build a medical clinic and store. The idea was passed down to the next superintendent Charles Thomson, and he delicately and successfully implemented the sensitive agenda. The Yosemite were relocated to new cabin houses in 1933 and they were charged rent and utilities.[54] According to national park historian Mark Spence, Thomson's removal strategy was to cancel the lease and forfeit the right of residence if the Yosemite fell delinquent in their payments or absent from their home for too long. Moreover, even though the Yosemite were employed by the park, they would eventually lose the lease once they retired and were unable to pay the bills. By the 1940s, the number of Yosemite residents was cut in half. Once vacated, the houses were burned by park officials to prevent the influx of new residents. By the late 1960s, the park officials had destroyed all the cabins except one, which they converted into a management office.[55]

The genesis of Yosemite as a state and national park, therefore, is a dark one: military campaigns authorized by the federal and California governments subdued the Indigenous peoples, commercial interests and profit-making wore the guise of nature conservation, Indigenous culture was exploited for tourism development, and Indigenous peoples were deceived and, ultimately, removed altogether. Even though the colonial invasions committed by Columbus and the birth of state parks are two separate events at least a few centuries apart, the gist of these events are not so different after all.

The State Park Movement

After the establishment of Indian Spring Reserve and Yosemite Valley, several state parks began to emerge across the United States during the late 19th century and early 20th centuries.[56] These state parks include Niagara Falls

Reservation (est. 1883) and Adirondack and Catskill Forest Preserves (est. 1885) in New York; Itasca State Park in Minnesota (est. 1891); Mackinac Island State Park in Michigan (est. 1895)[57]; Interstate State Park in Minnesota (est. 1895) and Wisconsin (est. 1900)[58]; and Big Redwoods Basin State Park in California (est. 1902).

Despite the establishment of these state parks, there was no concerted effort to build state parks on the national scale, and it was more or less "the here-and-there valiant efforts of idealists."[59] However, the first half of the 20th century was perfect timing for the expansion of state park systems since the demand for nature preservation and outdoor recreation was as strong as ever, and long-distance travel emerged as a popular American pastime, due to the availability of affordable automobiles and the expansion of road and highway systems.[60]

During this time, Stephen T. Mather, the first director of the National Park Service (NPS), played an instrumental role in the formation of the state park movement, a coherent nationwide effort to create state parks across different states. Mather was an avid outdoorsman, environmentalist, and millionaire who made his fortune through a mining business in Chicago. His career with the Department of the Interior and the NPS began with his letter to Secretary of the Interior Franklin K. Lane in 1914. In the letter, Mather deplored the deteriorating natural conditions of several national parks and criticized the federal government's indifference and the Department of the Interior's poor management.[61] Lane was intrigued by Mather's enthusiasm, as he was looking for a replacement for his assistant, Adolph Miller. Lane met with Mather for the first time in Chicago and again in Washington, D.C.[62] Lane explained to Mather that the existing eight national parks were "orphans," because their administration was split among three different departments (War, Agriculture, and Interior). He stressed that Mather's main job was to lobby Congress to create a central administrative unit for the parks.[63] Mather eventually accepted the position with one condition: He would stay for only one year. He stayed for more than a decade.

With his exceptional public relations skills, Mather successfully navigated Washington politics and played an instrumental role in the creation of the NPS in 1916. Mather even used his own money to campaign for national parks: As a billionaire who was passionate about nature preservation and outdoor recreation, he was not restricted by the small salary allocated by the federal government. In the following year, Mather became the first director of the newly created agency.[64]

But his aggressive and successful promotion of national parks also created a problem. Soon after becoming the director of the agency, Mather was inundated with numerous requests from zealous park advocates to create national parks in their states. Mather thought that most of the proposed park areas were not spectacular of national significance, and believed that national parks must contain truly exceptional and magnificent natural beauty. As a solution, he envisioned that, instead of focusing on creating more national parks, each state could create its own park system for the environmental protection and recreation of state residents.[65] Subsequently, Mather, Judge John Barton Payne (later Secretary of the Interior), and Iowa Governor William L. Harding organized the National Conference on Parks, the first national meeting to discuss the ideology, provision, and management of state parks. It was held on January 10, 1921, and Des Moines, Iowa was selected as the conference location because the state had made noticeable progress in state park development.[66]

Although the conference garnered considerable interest and was attended by more than 200 delegates from 24 states and the District of Columbia, it was planned in a rather haphazard manner. Most attendees did not know exactly what they would be doing at the conference and they soon discovered a conspicuous inconsistency in the concept of state parks among themselves. National parks were primarily focused on preserving wilderness conditions to provide an immersive nature experience; this made their site selection and choice of infrastructure and recreational facilities more restrictive. State parks, on the other hand, were pretty much in the hands of each state. Because of the lack of uniform design and management principles, state parks in the early 20th century varied in scenic quality, landscape modification, and infrastructure, some of them including man-made lakes, playgrounds, tennis courts, baseball fields, and even golf courses.[67]

Despite the lack of organization, clear agendas, and coherent opinions, the conference accomplished several milestones for the state park movement. Mather expressed his desire to help develop stronger state park systems across the country and acknowledged that the NPS could provide support for planning, fundraising, wildlife management, and marketing of state parks within each state.[68] Although their opinions varied, conference attendees were able to identify and summarize their common beliefs regarding the identity and management principle of state parks.[69] A conference slogan "A State Park Every Hundred Miles" emerged, capturing the park advocates' enthusiasm for expanding state park systems throughout the nation.[70] The conference attendees agreed to form the National Conference on State Parks (NCSP) which would serve as a central forum for state park professionals until 1974, when it was split into the National Association of State Park Directors and the National Society for Park Resources.[71] By 1926, these efforts resulted in 43 of the 48 states establishing either state parks or state forests entirely or partially devoted to recreational use.[72] The National Conference on Parks in 1921 marked the beginning of the nationwide state park movement in the U.S.

Broken Promise of Democratic Access

One of the most emphasized topics during the National Conference on Parks was democratic access to state parks, so much so that it was articulated in the third of the 11 conference resolutions:

That it is incumbent upon our government, local, country, state and national, to continue to acquire sites suitable for recreation and the preservation of wild life, until eventually there shall be public parks within *easy access of all the people of our nation* [emphasis added].[73]

A few years later, a nearly identical statement was adopted as the mission of the NCSP, which states that the purpose of the organization is to enhance the people's access to parks by urging federal, state, and municipal governments to create more state parks.[74] This emphasis on the accessibility of state parks was understandable because, by and large, visiting wilderness, forests, and vast natural areas was still a leisure activity of upper-class Americans during the early 20th century. For example, Jens Jensen, a Danish-American landscape architect based in Chicago, pointed out during the first conference that national parks are located in remote places and most Americans do not have enough money to visit them.[75] Democratic access served as a core mission of the state park movement from the very beginning.

There was a distressing divergence, however, between the repeated emphasis on democratic access to state parks and the reality that was playing out in the country. When park leaders explicated the democratic ideal of state parks, Jim Crow laws and customs were being solidified across the nation, particularly in the South, and African Americans had extremely limited opportunities to visit state parks.[76] The "separate but equal" doctrine established by the Supreme Court decision in *Plessy v. Ferguson* in 1896 set clear boundaries pertaining to where African Americans could visit and what they could do during their leisure time.[77] By 1940, only seven state parks were available for African Americans across 15 Southern states. One of the first state parks in the South was Mount Mitchell State Park in North Carolina established in 1915. Yet, the state did not create a state park for African Americans until it built Jones Lake State Park in 1939, despite African Americans constituting approximately 30% of the state population from 1910 to 1940.[78]

According to William O'Brien, there were two types of state parks for African Americans during the Jim Crow era: (1) Standalone parks built in entirely different locations from White parks and (2) Dual-use system parks adjacent to White parks. In either case, African American parks were almost always smaller, farther away from the cities, in lower-quality locations, poorly maintained, and rudimentary in their day-use-only facilities. The lack of standardization in state park design and infrastructure worked against African Americans' access to state parks, because such ambiguity allowed the Southern states to turn pretty much any poor-quality land into state parks for African Americans. Moreover, the dual-use parks ensured the greatest degree of racial separation, including separate access roads for Whites and Blacks as well as tracts of forest, lakes, and ponds to demarcate racial segregation.[79]

Although the state park movement gained unprecedented momentum during the 1930s and 40s from the Civilian Conservation Corps (CCC) program, park provision for African Americans was very sluggish. From its inception during the Great Depression in 1933 to its dissolution in 1942, CCC programs employed approximately two million young men in America and helped build 711 state parks and 46 federal RDAs, most of which were later designated as state parks.[80] Despite such unprecedented support for state park provision, McKay's study documented that in nine southern states in 1952, there were 180 state parks available to Whites, while only 12 were available to African Americans—15 times more state parks for Whites than Blacks.[81] Yet, the inequality between the two groups is even more astonishing in the size of actual parklands: While Whites had 986,184 acres of parklands, African Americans had only 8,879 acres, which is a mere 0.9% of what the former had.[82] Adding to these staggering statistics of park inequality is the fact that during the 1930s and 1940s, nearly 80% of the African American population in the U.S. resided in the South.[83]

White Southerners' racism was the culprit of the park disparity. From the beginning of the CCC program, the NPS not only controlled the allocation of CCC labor, but also provided consultative and advisory assistance to the park planning and construction.[84] However, when the NPS officials tried to create more state parks exclusively for African Americans in the South, they were met with indifference, ignorance, and resistance from local White politicians, park officials, and community members. According to O'Brien, the NPS could not push the agency's nondiscriminatory policy harder, because it had to navigate the delicate political landscape at the local level. Even though the NPS officials occasionally increased the pressure to create more African American state parks, Southern states almost always responded by turning cheap and poor-quality lands into African American parks. In the end, most of the sites allocated for Black parks ended up in the hands of White Americans or were abandoned altogether.[85]

Several NPS officials were frustrated by the lack of progress in state park provision for African Americans. In 1937, Fred T. Johnston, who worked under Conard Wirth, wrote a letter to NPS director Arno B. Cammerer and expressed his frustration with how the Southern states continued to curtail the agency's effort to provide RDAs to African Americans. R. C. Robinson, a NPS recreation planner in Region I, was equally disgruntled: He too had witnessed several occasions when planned park facilities for African Americans never materialized.[86] In his influential book, *An American Dilemma: The Negro Problem and Modern Democracy*, the Nobel Prize winner Gunnar Myrdal observed that, in the South, beaches, playgrounds, and public parks "are often entirely closed to Negroes" and "the Southern whites are unconcerned about how Negroes use their leisure time, as long as they are kept out of the whites' parks and beaches."[87]

It is important to highlight that, despite their lack of access to state parks, many African Americans participated in the CCC program and made significant contributions to the state park movement. Although Robert Fechner, the first director of the CCC program, resisted hiring Blacks in administrative positions, approximately 250,000 African Americans participated in the program and were assigned to Black CCC units to create or renovate state and national parks across the nation.[88] Those Black CCC members were essentially creating White parks that they could not use because of Jim Crow laws and customs. For example, when Millard Fillmore Rutherford, a former Black CCC member at Fort Parker State Park in Texas, returned to show his bride the park, they were told that African Americans were not allowed to enter the park.[89]

While state parks reserved for African Americans in the South were extremely rare and inferior in terms of functionality and aesthetic value, the situation in the North was not particularly better. One of the biggest misconceptions about the racial relationship in the U.S. is that institutional racism against African Americans was limited to the South and Jim Crow Era. The truth is that African Americans endured racism in employment, housing, education, social services, and politics throughout the nation.[90] In Michigan, for example, racial discrimination was common at all parks and recreation facilities during the 1960s, and state parks were located in White-dominated rural communities, making it very challenging for African Americans to visit and enjoy them safely.[91]

The Chicago Defender documented at least three separate incidents of racial discrimination against people of color at Indiana Dunes State Park in Indiana during the 1930s. On June 9th, a group of schoolteachers of color "experienced some insults at the hands of some employees" during their picnic at the park. About a month later, when a group of African Americans planned a picnic at the improved facilities at the park, they were directed by the park officials to use a section that was "not improved sufficiently for the protection of the health and lives of the public." The party submitted formal complaints, and Governor Paul V. McNutt ordered an investigation of the park's discrimination. Yet, in 1937, when several youths of color used public bathing beaches at the park, they were ordered by park officials to use the extreme end of the beach and told that Jim Crow segregation is the rule of the park. Frustrated by the mistreatment, the group demanded meetings with the park board commission to understand when and how the rule was established.[92]

In the Adirondack Park in New York in 1932, a Black man living in the forest was chased down and shot to death under dubious circumstances. Two residents of Indian Lake, Ernie Blanchard and Lester Turner, encountered the Black man in the woods and later filed a complaint with the authorities. Existing records do not clearly show the nature of their first encounter and the complaint, yet the situation somehow evolved into a manhunt by a group of nine White men consisting of local residents, police officers, and state troopers. The group eventually killed the Black man in a gunfight, and his identity and life story are still a mystery. Despite the lack of evidence, the Black man had been "dehumanized as an animal, pathologized as a lunatic, and criminalized as a burglar."[93] A journalist who interviewed the White men in the 1970s was told that the Black man was "a huge creature covered with hair from head to foot" so the journalist later described the man as an "Adirondack Bigfoot," while the autopsy record shows that he was only five feet, six inches tall and 130 pounds.[94] Because of the conspicuous lack of supporting evidence provided by survivors showing the legitimacy of the manhunting and killing, the historian Eliza Darling claimed any rational reader would conclude the man was murdered by "a lynch mob" rather than the law.[95]

In Heckscher State Park in Suffolk County, New York in 1940, a complaint was filed by E. L. Sullinger, a World War veteran, to NAACP Secretary Walter White, requesting a formal investigation of racial segregation practices at the park. Sullinger explained that he received a copy of park rules from the Long Island State Park Commission showing that organized groups wishing to use certain parks must secure an application five days before the visit. The rules also noted that organized groups need to report to the park superintendent immediately upon arrival to be assigned to a certain area, and all members of the group must confine their activities to the assigned areas. Sullinger argued that "This ruling, while it appears innocent enough, permits the Commission to segregate negroes or anyone else that does not suit the fancy of certain people." Later, Thurgood Marshall on the special council of NAACP shared the information with Lieutenant Governor Charles Poletti.[96]

It is important to note that state parks were not the only recreation sites where African Americans' recreational needs were unmet. Although the recreation movement emerged during the early 20th century to provide wholesome recreation programs to underprivileged urban youth, the recreation needs of African Americans were simply ignored.[97] Recreational facilities such as theme parks, theaters, pool halls, swimming pools, beaches, resorts, playgrounds, and recreation and sport centers were either segregated or severely scarce for Black citizens.[98] Moreover, the rise of the Ku Klux Klan and the lynching of Black people in the woods instigated a considerable fear of the wildlands and nature-based outdoor recreation within generations of African American communities.[99] They had to rely on travel guidebooks such as *The Negro Motorist Green Book* to avoid humiliation or, worse, life-threatening racism during leisure travel.[100]

With their leisure opportunities deprived by Jim Crow laws and practices in the country, African Americans employed two distinctive strategies to claim their parks and recreation. First, African Americans carved out their own recreation space by creating amusement parks, pool rooms, theaters, and dance halls operated exclusively for African Americans.[101] Similarly, Black entrepreneurs and civic leaders built nature resorts exclusively for African Americans. Some of those Black resorts include Buckroe Beach in Virginia, Idlewild in Michigan, Gulfside Assembly in Mississippi, Highland Beach in Maryland, and Lincoln Hills in Colorado.[102] Black sport organizations, such as the Negro Leagues, American Tennis Association, and United Golfers Association were also formed.[103] These efforts to create African Americans' own leisure space are consistent with what Darlene Hine described as the creation of parallel institutions, professional organizations for Black doctors, nurses, and lawyers that represent remarkable Black agency and resistance during the age of Jim Crow.[104]

Another strategy of African Americans was direct legal confrontation with racist policies and practices. From the 1940s to the 1960s, civil rights activists and organizations filed numerous lawsuits across the nation to challenge "the separate but equal" doctrine.[105] The NAACP and the Legal Defense and Educational Fund (a civil rights organization that originated from the legal department of NAACP) were at the forefront of the desegregation effort of southern state parks. The organizations provided legal support to African American plaintiffs and demanded full desegregation of state parks across the South. But park officials in these states were not willing to give way to desegregation. Even though the Supreme Court case of *Brown v. Board of Education of Topeka, Kansas* in 1954 ruled that racial segregation in public education violated the 14th Amendment and was therefore unconstitutional, only a few states (such as Maryland, West Virginia, and Kentucky) promptly followed the ruling and desegregated their state parks. Other states intentionally delayed the legal process, ignored the court decisions citing local racial hostility, tried to sell the parkland to a private entity, and/or simply closed the park.[106]

Nevertheless, the perseverance of African American citizens and civil rights activists gradually came to fruition in the 1960s. After the turbulent years of legal battles and protests, Jim Crow segregation in state parks came to an official end when Seashore State Park (currently First Landing State Park) in Virginia reopened as a desegregated park in 1967.[107] Since the beginning of the state park movement in the 1920s, it took nearly a half-century for people of color to gain equal and democratic access to state parks in the U.S.

Racial Oppression in State Parks Die Hard

> We were made to feel that our struggle was unworthy of justice, that we were less than the whites, that we weren't fully Americans. We were shown that in the United States, not all men were equal under the law. We were shown that when Black voices called out for justice, no one cared.... . All we are asking for is a chance to be treated like a first-class citizen who truly is a beneficiary of the promise that this is a land where there is a "liberty and justice for all."
> Hughes Van Ellis at Capitol Hill in Washington D.C.
> on May 19, 2021.[108]

Hughes Van Ellis's statement could be a perfect summary of African Americans' experience with Jim Crow and racial discrimination in state parks, yet it is not about state parks or any public parks. Instead, it was his testimony as a survivor of the Tulsa-Greenwood Race Massacre in Oklahoma in 1921. The Massacre is often erroneously labeled as a "race riot" even though it was a large-scale act of terrorism against African

Americans, committed by White mobs under the auspices of state and local law enforcement authorities. White mobs destroyed more than 36 square blocks of Greenwood community, one of the wealthiest African American neighborhoods in the nation, famously known as Black Wall Street. They killed as many as 300 Black residents, burned 23 churches, rendered nearly 1,000 families homeless, and caused property damages equivalent to $32~$47 million in 2020 USD.[109]

Remarkably, the Tulsa-Greenwood Race Massacre unfolded approximately five months after the National Conference on Parks. In other words, in Des Moines, Iowa in January 1921, White park leaders in this country assembled and agreed to expand state park systems for the benefit of all Americans, yet just months later in Tulsa, Oklahoma, White mobs perpetrated one of the most egregious acts of racial violence in American history. Interestingly, the tale of these seemingly disparate events peculiarly converge in terms of generational trauma and pain of people of color.

For example, Albright and colleagues discovered a profound aftermath of the Massacre which has extended far beyond its time and location. The Massacre significantly worsened the homeownership rate and occupational status among Black Tulsans, yet it was widely circulated through newspapers, instilling fear among other Black communities that they could face similarly violent attacks. The researchers found that the Massacre had negatively impacted Black homeownership across the nation—an adverse effect that persisted well into the year 2000. It means that the devastating impact of the Massacre on Black individuals spilled over to other places in the U.S. and followed generations of African Americans.[110] Even today, victims of the Massacre, including Van Ellis, are still fighting for just reparation, since years of litigations against the state and city government have led nowhere. The racial violence committed more than a century ago is still haunting Black communities.

Similarly, Black exclusion and disfranchisement in state parks have stubbornly persisted. Although democratic access has been the backbone of the state park movement, Jim Crow laws erected considerable challenges for African Americans seeking access to the parks, particularly in the South where the majority of African Americans resided. Although the Civil Rights Act of 1964 outlawed discrimination in access to public facilities and services, years of racial discrimination had already deprived generations of African Americans the opportunities to cultivate cultural disposition, environmental attitude, and recreation knowledge and skills for appreciating parks and the great outdoors.[111] As a result, today's state park visitors are dominated by White Americans, as illustrated in the following visitor statistics:

- Michigan: In 1985, African Americans represented a mere 0.1% of state park visitors while they comprised 13% of the state population.[112]
- Missouri: A study conducted in 2005–06 reported that African Americans comprised only 0.6% of the total visitors of five different state parks while

they made up 11% of Missourians. White Americans comprised 94.5% of the total visitors.[113]
- Maryland: African Americans represented just 2.2% of day visitors to the state parks in 2010, while Whites represented 77.2%.[114]
- Georgia: A visitor study from three state parks in 2010 showed that Blacks and Latinos accounted for 6.1% and 5.7% of the total visitors observed at the parks' trailheads, respectively, while Whites constituted 82.2%.[115]
- Minnesota: Non-Whites were only 5% of state park visitors in 2017 although they were nearly 20% of the state population.[116]

Thus, the Tulsa-Greenwood Race Massacre and the American state park movement are events of the past, but their detrimental effects are far from over. Jim Crow ended more than a half-century ago, yet it continues to cast a long shadow over communities of color.

The history of state parks is a history of American colonialism, capitalism, and racism. It's a history of robbing Indigenous lands, forcibly removing Indigenous peoples, and excluding and exploiting African Americans. As the previous and current chapters vividly depict, community and urban parks and state parks share a troubling history of violence and oppression toward vulnerable and marginalized groups. More disturbing is that this dark history of American public parks is far from over. The next chapter of this book unearths another thick layer of injustice that has been laid beneath the birth of national parks in the United States.

Notes

1 William E O'Brien, *Landscapes of exclusion: State parks and Jim Crow in the American South* (University of Massachusetts Press, 2016), 7.
2 W. J. Faulkner, [Letter to Sam Brewster], 1937.
3 Rebecca Conard, "The National Conference on State Parks: Reflections on Organizational Genealogy" (paper presented at the The George Wright Forum, 1997); George Bennett, "The National Park Conference at Des Moines, Iowa, January 10-11-12, 1921," *Iowa Conservation* 5 (1921); Ney C. Landrum, *The State Park Movement in America: A Critical Review* (University of Missouri Press, 2004); Freeman Tilden, *The State Parks: Their Meaning in American Life* (Alfred A. Knopf, 1962).
4 For RDA, see Harlan D. Unrau and G. Frank Williss, *Administrative History: Expansion of the National Park Service in the 1930s* (National Park Service, 1983). https://www.nps.gov/parkhistory/online_books/unrau-williss/adhi.htm; O'Brien, *Landscapes of Exclusion*, 6.
5 Lary M. Dilsaver, *America's National Park System: The Critical Documents* (Rowman & Littlefield, 2016); Linda W. Greene, *Yosemite, the Park and Its Resources: A History of the Discovery, Management, and Physical Development of Yosemite National Park, California: Historical Narrative*, vol. 1 (U.S. Department of the Interior, 1987); Alfred Runte, *Yosemite: The Embattled Wilderness* (University of Nebraska Press, 1990).
6 Margaret Beauchamp Armistead, "Chief William McIntosh and the Indian Springs Treaties," *The Georgia Review* 11, no. 3 (1957).
7 Landrum, *The State Park Movement in America*, 36. An assemblyman William Y. Baker introduced the bill "to provide for a state park in the state of Wisconsin" (An Act to provide for a state park in the state of Wisconsin, 1878). The goal was to set apart 480,000 acres of land located in today's Vilas and Iron Counties as a state-owned park to prevent "cut[ing] down or destroy[ing] of any timber growing on such lands." See Vernon Carstensen, *Farms or Forests: Evolution of State Land Policy for Northern Wisconsin, 1850–1932* (College of Agriculture, University of Wisconsin, 1958), 15. Thus, the emphasis was placed on the protection of natural resources within the land rather than recreational use. Today, the park does not exist, because the state sold the land to lumber companies in 1897. See George Rogers, "The might-have-been State Park," *Wisconsin Natural Resources* 19, no. 6 (December 1995).
8 Roxanne Dunbar-Ortiz, *An Indigenous Peoples' History of the United States* (Beacon Press, 2014); Roxanne Dunbar-Ortiz, *Not "a Nation of Immigrants": Settler Colonialism, White Supremacy, and a History of Erasure and Exclusion* (Beacon Press, 2021).
9 James W. Loewen, *Lies My Teacher Told Me: Everything Your American History Textbook Got Wrong* (The New Press, 2018), Chapter 2; Howard Zinn, *A People's History of the United States* (HarperCollins, 2015), Chapter 1.
10 Loewen, *Lies My Teacher Told Me*, 53–60.
11 Bartolomé de La Casas, *History of the Indies. Translated and Edited by Andrée Collard* (Harper and Row, 1971), 154.
12 Dunbar-Ortiz, *An Indigenous Peoples' History of the United States*; Anton Treuer, *The Indian Wars: Battles, Bloodshed, and the Fight for Freedom on the American Frontier* (National Geographic, 2016).

13 Dunbar-Ortiz, *An Indigenous Peoples' History of the United States*. For military forts, see Mark David Spence, *Dispossessing the Wilderness: Indian Removal and the Making of the National Parks* (Oxford University Press, 1999), 29.
14 Dorceta E. Taylor, *The Rise of the American Conservation Movement: Power, Privilege, and Environmental Protection* (Duke University Press, 2016), 113.
15 Arthur Spirling, "US treaty making with American Indians: Institutional change and relative power, 1784–1911," *American Journal of Political Science* 56, no. 1 (2012).
16 Vine Deloria and Raymond J. DeMallie, *Documents of American Indian Diplomacy: Treaties, Agreements, and Conventions, 1775–1979* (University of Oklahoma Press, 1999), 6.
17 Dunbar-Ortiz, *Not "a Nation of Immigrants."*
18 Jason Byrne and Jennifer Wolch, "Nature, race, and parks: past research and future directions for geographic research," *Progress in Human Geography* 33, no. 6 (2009); Denis Cosgrove, "Habitable earth: Wilderness, empire, and race in America," in *Wild Ideas*, ed. D. Rothenberg (University of Minnesota Press, 1995); KangJae Jerry Lee et al., "Slow violence in public parks in the U.S.: can we escape our troubling past?," *Social & Cultural Geography* 24, no. 7 (2023); Lee et al., "Slow violence in public parks in the U.S."
19 Christine Park Hankinson, "Indian Springs," *The Georgia Review* 1, no. 4 (1947).
20 Robbie Ethridge, *Creek Country: The Creek Indians and Their World* (University of North Carolina Press, 2004).
21 Armistead, "Chief William McIntosh."; Hankinson, "Indian Springs."
22 Armistead, "Chief William McIntosh."; Hankinson, "Indian Springs." For the information on the inn, see Andrew K. Frank, "The Rise and Fall of William McIntosh: Authority and Identity on the Early American Frontier," *The Georgia Historical Quarterly* 86, no. 1 (2002): 29–30.
23 Armistead, "Chief William McIntosh"; Hankinson, "Indian Springs"; Frank, "The Rise and Fall of William McIntosh."
24 Frank, "The Rise and Fall of William McIntosh," 36, 44, 47; Armistead, "Chief William McIntosh."
25 Michael D. Green, *The Politics of Indian Removal: Creek Government and Society in Crisis* (University of Nebraska Press, 1982), 75, 81, 82.
26 Green, *The Politics of Indian Removal* 81–82, 87–91.
27 For the quote, see Armistead, "Chief William McIntosh," 313; Hankinson, "Indian Springs"; Green, *The Politics of Indian Removal*, 96.
28 Green, *The Politics of Indian Removal*, 117–22. Although the terms of the 1826 Treaty of Washington were far more favorable to the Creeks than those of the previous treaty, their relocation process was not smooth and the conflict between the state of Georgia and the federal government emerged. For more information, see chapter 6 as well as Richard J. Hryniewicki, "The Creek Treaty of November 15, 1827," *The Georgia Historical Quarterly* 52, no. 1 (1968).
29 For the Georgia legislature, see Armistead, "Chief William McIntosh." For the renaming, see General Assembly of Georgia, Acts of the General Assembly of the state of Georgia, passed in Milledgeville at an annual session in November and December, 1827 [volume 1] 1827, https://hdl.handle.net/2027/nyp.33433001215882.
30 Greene, *Yosemite, the Park and Its Resource*, 1, 1–2.

31 Francis Peloubet Farquhar, *Exploration of the Sierra Nevada* (California Historical Society, 1925), 6. For a more rigorous historical reconstruction, see Scott Stine, *A Way Across the Mountain: Joseph Walker's 1833 Trans-Sierran Passage and the Myth of Yosemite's Discovery* (University of Oklahoma Press, 2015).
32 Shirley Sargent, *Wawona's Yesterdays* (Yosemite Natural History Association, 1961), 64.
33 Annie R. Mitchell, "Major James D. Savage and the Tularenos," *California Historical Society Quarterly* 28, no. 4 (1949).
34 Greene, *Yosemite, the Park and Its Resource*, 1, 17–18; Mitchell, "Major James D. Savage."
35 Greene, *Yosemite, the Park and Its Resource*, 1, 19, 23.
36 Greene, *Yosemite, the Park and Its Resource*, 24; Runte, *Yosemite*, 11; Lafayette Houghton Bunnell, *Discovery of the Yosemite, and the Indian War of 1851, Which Led to that Event* (New York: Fleming H. Revell Company, 1892), 147; Elizabeth Godfrey, *Yosemite Indians* (Yosemite Association, 1977), 10.
37 Greene, *Yosemite, the Park and Its Resource*, 1, 24–25.
38 For early Yosemite visitors, see Greene, *Yosemite, the Park and Its Resource*, 32–35.
39 James Mason Hutchings, *In the Heart of the Sierras: The Yo Semite Valley, Both Historical and Descriptive: And Scenes by the Way* (Pacific Press, Publishing House, 1886), 130.
40 Runte, *Yosemite*, 19.
41 Hank Johnston, "Yosemite: The first National Park," *Yosemite Association* 61, no. 3 (1999).
42 David Vogel, "Business Support for Nature Protection in the Nineteenth Century," *Journal of Policy History* 34, no. 2 (2022).
43 Joseph H. Engbeck, *State Parks of California, from 1864 to the Present* (C.H. Belding, 1980), 19.
44 For Olmsted's view on Yosemite, see John F. Sears, *Sacred Places: American Tourist Attractions in the Nineteenth Century* (Oxford University Press, 1989), 130; Johnston, "Yosemite: The first National Park."
45 Johnston, "Yosemite: The first National Park."; Greene, *Yosemite, the Park and Its Resource*, 1, 52.
46 Vogel, "Business Support for Nature Protection in the Nineteenth Century."
47 Runte, *Yosemite*, 19–21.
48 Spence, *Dispossessing the Wilderness*, 103–04.
49 Edward D. Castillo, "Petition to Congress on Behalf of the Yosemite Indians," *The Journal of California Anthropology* 5, no. 2 (1978): 273.
50 Runte, *Yosemite*, 49, 54–55.
51 Runte, *Yosemite*, 144.
52 Spence, *Dispossessing the Wilderness*, 117.
53 Spence, *Dispossessing the Wilderness*, 120.
54 Spence, *Dispossessing the Wilderness*, 122–123.
55 Spence, *Dispossessing the Wilderness*, 123–130.
56 Tilden, *The State Parks*, 5–7; Landrum, *The State Park Movement in America*, 35–46; Thomas R. Cox, *The Park Builders: A History of State Parks in the Pacific Northwest* (University of Washington Press, 1988), 4–5.
57 Mackinac Island State Park was initially established as Mackinac National Park in 1875, the second national park in the U.S. Unlike other early national parks, Mackinac was under the jurisdiction of the War Department, because Fort

Mackinac was already established on the island. It became the first state park in Michigan in 1895. For more information, see Keith R. Widder, *Mackinac National Park, 1875–1895* (Mackinac Island State Park Commission, 1975).

58 Interstate State Park was the outcome of interstate collaboration between Minnesota and Wisconsin to make a state park. The Minnesota side of the park was completed first. Another example of interstate collaboration is Palisades Interstate Park in New Jersey and New York (est. 1900). See Mary Laine, "Interstate State Park," *MNopedia* (2016). https://www.mnopedia.org/place/interstate-state-park; Landrum, *The State Park Movement in America*, 51, 55; Tilden, *The State Parks*, 118.

59 Tilden, *The State Parks*, 5.

60 Landrum, *The State Park Movement in America*, 72.

61 Horace M. Albright and Marian Albright Schenck, *Creating the National Park Service: The Missing Years* (University of Oklahoma Press, 1999), 30.

62 There is a popular story that Mather and Lane had known each other since their college years at U.C. Berkeley and Mather took the Interior job after receiving a response letter from Lane: "Dear Steve: If you don't like the way the national parks are run, why don't you come down to Washington and run them yourself?" However, Horace Albright, assistant of Mather and later the 2nd Director of the NPS, explained that the story is not true and the two did not know each other. See *Creating the National Park Service*, 32.

63 Albright and Albright Schenck, *Creating the National Park Service*, 35.

64 Robert Shankland, *Steve Mather of the National Parks* (New York: Alfred A. Knopf, 1976), Chapter 5.

65 Tilden, *The state parks*, 3; Landrum, *The State Park Movement in America*, 76; Conard, "The National Conference on State Parks," 30.

66 Bennett, "The National Park Conference" 14; Conard, "The National Conference on State Parks."; Landrum, *The State Park Movement in America*, 81.

67 Landrum, *The State Park Movement in America*, 82–84; Tilden, *The State Parks*, 8; Conard, "The National Conference on State Parks," 31; O'Brien, *Landscapes of Exclusion*, 21–22.

68 Tilden, *The State Parks*, 13; Landrum, *The State Park Movement in America*, 85–86.

69 Conard, "The National Conference on State Parks," 35; Bennett, "The National Park Conference" 24.

70 Tilden, *The State Parks*, 8.

71 Conard, "The National Conference on State Parks," 28.

72 Raymond H. Torrey, *State Parks and Recreational Uses of State Forests in the United States*, The National Conference on State Parks (Washington, D.C., 1926), 9.

73 Bennett, "The National Park Conference" 24.

74 Torrey, *State Parks and Recreational Uses of State Forests in the United States*, 25.

75 Bennett, "The National Park Conference" 18.

76 O'Brien, *Landscapes of Exclusion*.

77 The catalyst for the landmark U.S. Supreme Court decision was Homer Plessy, a mixed-race man, who intentionally sat in a Whites-only train car in New Orleans, Louisiana in order to challenge the entire system of racial segregation in America. For more information, see Harvey Fireside, *Separate and Unequal: Homer Plessy and the Supreme Court Decision That Legalized Racism* (Basic Books, 2004); Steve Luxenberg, *Separate: The Story of Plessy v. Ferguson, and America's Journey from*

Slavery to Segregation (W.W. Norton & Company, 2019). For African Americans' leisure during Jim crow, see Andrew W. Kahrl and Malcolm Cammeron, *African American Outdoor Recreation* (U.S. Department of the Interior National Park Service, 2022); Myron F. Floyd and Rasul A. Mowatt, "Leisure among African Americans" in *Race, Ethnicity, and Leisure*, eds. Monika Stodolska et al. (Human Kinetics 2013); Victoria W. Wolcott, *Race, Riots, and Roller Coasters: The Struggle Over Segregated Recreation in America* (University of Pennsylvania Press, 2012).
78 O'Brien, *Landscapes of Exclusion*, 7, 61. For the African American population in North Carolina, see John Rodman Larkins, *The Negro Population of North Carolina: Social and Economic* (North Carolina State Board of Charities and Public Welfare, 1944).
79 O'Brien, *Landscapes of Exclusion*, 9, 7.
80 John C. Paige, *The Civilian Conservation Corps and the National Park Service, 1933–1942: An Administrative History* (National Park Service, US Department of the Interior, 1985), 131–32.
81 Robert B. McKay, "Segregation and public recreation," *Virginia Law Review* 40 (1954).
82 O'Brien, *Landscapes of Exclusion*, 14.
83 Campbell Gibson and Kay Jung, *Historical Census Statistics on Population Totals by Race, 1790 to 1990, and by Hispanic Origin, 1790 to 1990, for the United States, Regions, Divisions, and States* (Washington, D.C.: U.S. Census Bureau, 2002). The percentage was obtained by my calculations using the tables on pages 19 and 22.
84 Tilden, *The State Parks*, 13–14. Unrau and Williss, *Administrative History*, Chapter 3.
85 O'Brien, *Landscapes of Exclusion*, Chapter 3.
86 O'Brien, *Landscapes of Exclusion*, 77.
87 Gunnar Myrdal, *An American Dilemma: The Negro Problem and Modern Democracy* (Harper & Brothers, 1944), 346, 47.
88 For the discrimination in hiring, see Owen Cole Jr., *The African-American Experience in the Civilian Conservation Corps* (University Press of Florida, 1999), 21; Cynthia A. Brandimarte and Angela S. Reed, *Texas State Parks and the CCC: The Legacy of the Civilian Conservation Corps* (Texas A&M University Press, 2013), 52; Sarah M. Zaragoza, "The 3760: An African-American CCC Company" *Forest History Today* (Spring/Fall 2010).
89 Brandimarte and Reed, *Texas State Parks and the CCC*, 76–77.
90 Joe R. Feagin and Kimberley Ducey, *Racist America: Roots, Current Realities, and Future Reparations* (Routledge, 2018).
91 Patrick Cooper-McCann, "The Promise of Parkland: Planning Detroit's Public Spaces, 1805–2018" (Doctoral University of Michigan, 2019), 141.
92 "Indiana Governor to probe Dunes Park Jim Crow rule," *The Chicago Defender (National Edition)* June 30, 1934; "Bars bathers at beach in Indiana park," *The Chicago Defender (National Edition)* August 28, 1937.
93 Eliza Jane Darling, "The rest of the story, part 1," *Adirondack Daily Enterprise* (April 24, 2021). https://www.adirondackdailyenterprise.com/opinion/columns/you-know-what-local-history-by-howard-riley/2021/04/the-rest-of-the-story-part-1/.
94 Darling, "The rest of the story, part 1."

95 Eliza Jane Darling, "The rest of the story, part 2," *Adirondack Daily Enterprise* (May 1, 2021). https://www.adirondackdailyenterprise.com/opinion/columns/you-know-what-local-history-by-howard-riley/2021/05/the-rest-of-the-story-part-2/.
96 Letter from E.L. Sullinger to Walter White, June 30, 1940, Papers of the NAACP, Part 15: Segregation and Discrimination, Complaints and Responses, 1940–1955, Series B: Administrative Files, 001441-014-0414, Library of Congress.
97 James Fredrick Murphy, "Egalitarianism and separatism: a history of approaches in the provision of public recreation and leisure service for blacks, 1906–1972" (Ph.D. Oregon State University, 1972).
98 Kahrl and Cammeron, *African American Outdoor Recreation*; Forrester B. Washington, "Recreational facilities for the Negro," *The Annals of the American Academy of Political and Social Science* 140, no. 1 (1928); Wolcott, *Race, Riots, and Roller Coasters*.
99 Carolyn Finney, *Black Faces, White Spaces: Reimagining the Relationship of African Americans to the Great Outdoors* (UNC Press, 2014); Grace Elizabeth Hale, *Making Whiteness: The Culture of Segregation in the South, 1890–1940* (Vintage, 1999); Rasul A. Mowatt, "Lynching as leisure: Broadening notions of a field," *American Behavioral Scientist* 56, no. 10 (2012); Paul Outka, *Race and Nature from Transcendentalism to the Harlem Renaissance* (Palgrave Macmillan, 2016).
100 Derek H. Alderman, Kortney Williams, and Ethan Bottone, "Jim Crow journey stories: African American driving as emotional labor," *Tourism Geographies* 24, no. 2–3 (2022); Susan Sessions Rugh, "Vacation without Humiliation" in *Are We There Yet?: The Golden Age of American Family Vacations* (University Press of Kansas, 2008).
101 Washington, "Recreational facilities for the Negro."
102 Mark S. Foster, "In the face of 'Jim Crow': Prosperous blacks and vacations, travel and outdoor leisure, 1890–1945," *The Journal of Negro History* 84, no. 2 (1999); J. F. Hart, "A Rural Retreat for Northern Negroes," *The Geographical Review* 20, no. 2 (1960); Andrew W. Kahrl, *The Land Was Ours: African American Beaches from Jim Crow to the Sunbelt South* (Harvard University Press, 2012), 89–91; Josh, "Lincoln Hills Country Club," (September 20, 2017 2017). https://history.denverlibrary.org/news/african-american-research-library/lincoln-hills-country-club.
103 Neil Lanctot, *Negro League Baseball: The Rise and Ruin of a Black Institution* (University of Pennsylvania Press, 2008); Eric Allen Hall, *Arthur Ashe: Tennis and Justice in the Civil Rights Era* (Johns Hopkins University Press, 2014); Lane Demas, *Game of Privilege: An African American History of Golf* (The University of North Carolina Press, 2017).
104 Darlene Clark Hine, "Black professionals and race consciousness: origins of the civil rights movement, 1890–1950," *The Journal of American History* 89, no. 4 (2003).
105 Wolcott, *Race, Riots, and Roller Coasters*.
106 For the creation of Legal Defense and Educational Fund, see O'Brien, *Landscapes of Exclusion*, 98, 123. For Southern states' resistance to racial desegregation, see 134–44.
107 O'Brien, *Landscapes of Exclusion*, 147.

108 U.S. House of Representatives, *Continuing Injustice: The Centennial of the Tulsa-Greenwood Race Massacre. Hearings before the Subcommittee on the Constitution, Civil Rights, and Civil Liberties of the Committee on the Judiciary*, 13 (U.S. Government Publishing Office, May 19, 2021).

109 James S. Hirsch, *Riot and Remembrance: The Tulsa Race War and Its Legacy* (Houghton Mifflin Company, 2002), 226; Alex Albright et al., *After the Burning: The Economic Effects of the 1921 Tulsa Race Massacre*, National Bureau of Economic Research (2021), 1–3.

110 Albright et al., *After the Burning*.

111 Finney, *Black Faces, White Spaces*; Cassandra Y. Johnson and J. Michael Bowker, "African-American wildland memories," *Environmental Ethics* 26, no. 1 (2004); KangJae Jerry Lee and David Scott, "Bourdieu and African Americans' Park Visitation: The Case of Cedar Hill State Park in Texas," *Leisure Sciences* 38, no. 5 (2016).

112 Claire V. Korn, *Yesterday Through Tomorrow: Michigan State Parks* (Michigan State University Press, 1989), 77.

113 Daniel J. Witter, *Missouri Department of Natural Resources: State Park Visitor Study, 2005–2006* (Missouri Department of Natural Resources, 2007), 57.

114 Rebecca Dougherty, *2010 Maryland State Parks Economic Impact and Visitor Study* (Maryland Office of Tourism Development, 2011), 22.

115 Jason W. Whiting, Lincoln R. Larson, and Gary T. Green, "Monitoring visitation in Georgia state parks using the System for Observing Play and Recreation in Communities (SOPARC)," *Journal of Park and Recreation Administration* 30, no. 4 (2012): 27.

116 The Research Edge LLC, *2017 Minnesota State Parks Visitor Survey* (Minnesota Department of Natural Resources, 2017), 14, https://files.dnr.state.mn.us/about dnr/reports/parks/2017_state_parks_visitor_survey.pdf.

3 National Parks

There is nothing so American as our national parks. The scenery and wild life are native and the fundamental idea behind the parks is native. It is, in brief, that the country belongs to the people; that what it is in process of making is for the enrichment of the lives of all of us. Thus, the parks stand as the outward symbol of this great human principle.
Franklin D. Roosevelt, Radio Address from Two Medicine Chalet,
Glacier National Park, August 5, 1934[1]

…what a reservation is [sic], this is not land that was given to us by the United States[,] you know[,] if I go into your home and steal it from you[,] and then you fight back good enough to keep one of your bedrooms… .you know you would feel kinda like[,] I fought for that man[,] I kept this[,] I retained it[.] So this is [the] land that we retained[.] As a matter of fact where you are right now used to be part of our reservation…
Robert Hall, Two Medicine, Glacier National Park, at the
Native America Speaks program on June 29, 2019[2]

During his visit to Glacier National Park, Roosevelt exalted the natural beauty and cultural significance of not just Glacier but all the other U.S. national parks. FDR's radio address might have been personal because his fifth cousin and the 26th president of the United States, Theodore Roosevelt, played a critical role in the creation of national parks and millions of acres of other public lands such as national forests and nature reserves. For young Franklin Roosevelt, "Uncle Ted" was a hero, out West capturing desperadoes.[3] It is not coincidental that FDR's education and career trajectory mirrored those of Theodore. Indeed, similar to Teddy Roosevelt's conservation effort, FDR established the Civilian Conservation Corps program as a main part of his New Deal project during the Great Depression in 1933, hiring millions of unemployed young men for environmental and conservation projects to create or renovate national and state parks across the nation.[4]

DOI: 10.4324/9781032707624-5

Yet, 85 years after FDR stood on Two Medicine of Glacier National Park and declared national parks a symbol of democracy, Robert Hall stood on the same land and described the park as a symbol of oppression. He likened the U.S. government's displacement of the Glacier region Blackfeet to the theft of a home. To date, stories like Hall's have been a marginal voice in our discussion surrounding national parks because, for most Americans, the parks are not just sites of beautiful natural scenery and recreation, but places symbolizing distinctive national identity and patriotism, often venerated as "Crown jewels of America" and "the best idea we ever had."[5] But Hall is not alone in his assessment. Researchers have noted that the birth of U.S. national parks was marked by "imperialist, xenophobic, and racist features of American nationalism" because the parks were built through the ethnic cleansing of Indigenous peoples and the exclusion of the poor and people of color—a fact that Hall knew in his very blood as a Piikuni, one of six bands of the Blackfoot Confederacy who now live in the Blackfeet Indian Reservation next to Glacier National Park.[6]

This chapter unpacks the untold or poorly told stories surrounding the beginning of U.S. national parks and their developmental process. To this end, the chapter focuses on Yellowstone National Park in the West and Great Smoky Mountains and Shenandoah National Parks in the East. Unlike community and urban parks and state parks discussed in the previous chapters, national parks tend to entail larger parcels of land, contain more complex ecosystems, and attract more long-distance travelers. Yet, consistent with other types of public parks, U.S. national parks carry a troubling legacy of violence and oppression.

The Genesis of U.S. National Parks

It is difficult to point a specific event or individual responsible for the inception of U.S. national parks because their historical origins are complex, entailing various events in multiple locations. Most existing academic and popular writing highlights two specific events for the origin of the national park idea. First, George Catlin, a lawyer and self-taught painter of American Indians, is identified as the first person who articulated the national park vision. During the 1830s, Catlin took part in several trips to document the American Frontier and was deeply disturbed by what he perceived as the impending extinction of bison and American Indians. In his book published in 1841, *Letters and Notes on the Manners, Customs, and Condition of the North American Indian*, Catlin argued that "some great protecting policy of government" needs to be put in place to preserve "pristine beauty and wildness" in the western frontier:

> What a beautiful and thrilling specimen for America to preserve and hold up to the view of her refined citizens and the world, in future ages! A *nation's Park* [emphasis added], containing man and beast, in all the wild and freshness of their nature's beauty![7]

Another event often identified as a catalyst for national parks is the campfire discussion during the Washburn-Langford-Doane Expedition to Yellowstone in 1870. During the nineteen-man expedition consisting of prominent politicians, lawyers, reporters, and military personnel, the group had a discussion over a flickering campfire at Madison Junction regarding the best use of the land that they had surveyed. While one contingent proposed private development and commercial use of the land, Judge Cornelius Hedges rejected any private ownership and argued that the land should be set aside as a park protected by the federal government. All members of the expedition agreed with the idea.[8]

Exclusive attention to these two events and the heroization of a few White males might add a nice dramatic flourish, yet they can only provide an erroneous picture of the early history of national parks. No doubt that Catlin's idea and his use of the term "nation's Park" was innovative in his time. Yet, he was not alone in his disquiet with the fate of the American West. During the 19th century, White urban elites, journalists, artists, intellectuals, and political leaders were equally concerned with the mass-scale environmental destruction and overexploitation in the West, fearing that the frontier would eventually vanish.[9] Their collective concerns evolved into the American conservation and preservation movement, which served as a broader sociopolitical backdrop from which national parks emerged.[10]

The campfire story is romantic, but it is also apocryphal. The story has been widely celebrated by many generations of writers, historians, and even National Park Service (NPS) employees, yet prominent Yellowstone historians raised serious concerns about its credibility, pointing out that none of the original diaries, letters, or published articles by the Washburn party mentioned the campfire conversation.[11] Furthermore, the Folsom-Cook-Peterson expedition in 1869 had already explored Yellowstone, and Folsom directly communicated with Washburn about placing Yellowstone under federal protection.[12]

It is also tough to pin down which national park came first. Some sources claim that Hot Springs in Arkansas, the first National Reservation set aside in 1832, is essentially the first national park because it is recognized as the beginning of federal involvement in land management for recreational purposes.[13] Others argue that Yosemite should be considered the first, because the Yosemite Act in 1864 served as a model for the Yellowstone Act in 1872 and created the nation's first wildland park for preservation and public use.[14] Yellowstone National Park is widely recognized as the first national park because Yellowstone was placed under the jurisdiction of the Secretary of the Interior, which is under federal management. Yet, such a decision largely stemmed from the fact that Wyoming, where the majority of Yellowstone parkland was located, was not a state but a territory, and the park boundary extended to Montana and Idaho territories.[15] Indeed, "It is entirely possible that Congress may have preferred to make Yellowstone a state park in the same fashion as Yosemite" if there were no arguments over the park ownership between Wyoming and Montana territories.[16] Notably, by the time Yosemite was officially recognized as the third national park through the Yosemite Act in 1890 (Sequoia became the second national park only six days before Yosemite), the NPS did not even exist because the agency was established by the National Park Service Organic Act signed by Woodrow Wilson in 1916.[17]

Thus, these complexities surrounding national parks suggest that there is not a single, inspired, and inciting moment—a genesis—for the parks. Instead, similar to community and urban parks as well as state parks, the birth of national parks was not a coincidence but an outcome of the complex interplay of social, political, and cultural forces spanning the 19th and 20th centuries. While some of these forces, such as urbanization, industrialization, settler colonialism, capitalism, and ethnic cleansing have already been explained in previous chapters, there are two additional contexts imperative to the inception of national parks, namely environmental destruction and racist, sexist, and classist ideologies in the American conservation movement.

Environmental Destruction

Large-scale environmental destruction during the 19th century is a critical piece of the puzzle for how the U.S. national parks and other public parks came to be. Onslaughts of bison for economic profit,[18] railroad expansion, and industrialization led to the near extinction of much wildlife. Estimates showed that there were approximately 25 to 30 million bison in North America, and the number declined to less than 100 by the late 19th century.[19] Eastern pinnated grouse and the passenger pigeon were also on the brink of extinction, and both vanished by the early 20th century.[20] Americans also witnessed excessive commercial development in Niagara Falls from the early 1800s. Popular overlooks around the falls were purchased and gated by private owners as early as 1806, and by the mid-century "not a single point remained in the United States from which the falls could be viewed without paying the landowner a fee."[21] Construction of mills, tailraces, and conduits immediately adjacent to the river further despoiled Niagara Falls, making it a national embarrassment.[22]

Mounting criticism from European and domestic travelers to Niagara Falls only aggravated what Alfred Runte described as "cultural anxiety" or "cultural insecurity" that Americans had suffered for years.[23] Even though America's victory over Great Britain in the Revolutionary War was a big surprise to European powers, the new nation lacked a distinct cultural identity. Europeans trivialized American architecture, painting, literature, and music, and from their viewpoint, the disorderly situation in Niagara Falls was another example of the dearth of cultural sophistication among Americans. In this context, the rugged natural environment in the American Frontier emerged as an alternative to man-made marks of cultural achievement. Americans started to embrace wilderness as an authentic national character, something truly unique and absent in European countries.[24] Protecting the grandeur of the natural environment through government control, such as creating national parks, was a perfect opportunity for Americans to not only build a defining national character, but also to redeem themselves after the shame of Niagara Falls.[25]

In the meantime, environmental destruction was already well underway and had spread across major American cities. The cities grew exponentially due to industrial development, the influx of many immigrants, and urban migrants. As a result, the cities suffered from air and water pollution, sewage overload, epidemics, and poor sanitation. These urban conditions gave rise to romanticism and transcendentalism among urban elites and intellectuals, who started to conceive nature as an attractive, pristine, and healthy place—an antidote to urban problems.[26] Prominent transcendentalists such as Ralph Waldo Emerson and Henry David Thoreau offered extensive arguments about the beauty and healing properties of natural environments.[27] The American Frontier became a hot tourism destination for the rich and the powerful. Many American journalists wrote articles on the beauty of the American West, and artists such as Thomas Cole of the Hudson River School produced paintings capturing the grandeur of American wilderness as well as Indigenous peoples, fueling the nation's growing enthusiasm toward nature.[28] Gradually, Americans' collective environmental consciousness evolved into a broader social movement called the American conservation movement, a distinctive backdrop to the birth of national parks.

What is interesting about Americans' enthusiasm toward nature is that it was in direct opposition to the environmental attitudes of early European colonists and Euro-Americans during the 17th century. They were contemptuous and fearful of the vast natural environment in the North American continent because they had to not only tame the land through hard labor for survival but also protect themselves from dangerous wild animals and Indigenous peoples. To them, "nature" was nothing but a space of backbreaking labor and struggle for basic survival. Consistently, early texts describing the natural environment of the New World were filled with derogatory expressions often connoting biblical interpretations such as "barren and evil land," "distressing," "forbidding," "grim death," and "progress is God."[29]

In other words, during a few centuries, there was a drastic shift in Americans' collective idea of nature and wilderness, a transformation from something to be feared and frowned upon to something far more salubrious and desirable.[30] Once Americans started to gain more understanding and control over wild nature, their fear faded away and was gradually replaced by yearning. It means that American wilderness is very much a social and political construction. Americans needed wilderness, so they *invented* and *publicized* it.[31]

If anything, the shift in Americans' environmental attitudes serves as an acute reminder of one distinctive human nature: Self-serving interpretation of

66 *Violent and Verdant*

reality based on life circumstances and needs. One might argue that the shift is an indication of social advancement accomplished through scientific development. Another take, which I argue is a more just interpretation, might be the human ignorance and hypocrisy that have been recurring in our history. After all, Americans were busy destroying and removing wild nature for comfortable living and profits when it was abundant, but later they were eager to protect it once they made it scarce. "Ironically the very process that destroys wilderness stimulates its appreciation."[32]

Elitism, Racism, and Sexism in the American Conservation Movement

The birth of national parks can be understood as one of many outgrowths of the American conservation movement, a broad social and political effort that surfaced in the 19th century to preserve the natural environment and its resources. Although the movement emerged in response to the environmental destruction and rapid urbanization and industrialization, there is another motive at work: White elite conservation leaders' racist, sexist, and classist ideologies.[33] During the 19th century, White urban elites were increasingly alarmed by disappearing wildlife and Indigenous peoples and started to believe that the White race, themselves, may be similarly endangered. They wondered if the Nordic or White Americans could compete with a large number of immigrants and whether or not White social dominance would be maintained. They believed that if they failed, they, too, would vanish.[34]

In this context, conservationists began to apprehend the American Frontier as an important resource for White Americans, whom they believed were softened and spoiled by comfortable urban life, to regain tough and boisterous characters. During the post-Civil War era, elite men who came of age were "under intense pressure to embrace the cult of true manhood."[35] By linking wilderness with White supremacy and masculinity, the conservationists believed the White race in America could reinvigorate their aggression and machismo by subduing rugged wilderness or conquering primitive people. The Frontier was a perfect environment for elite young men to demonstrate their physical strength, endurance, self-reliance, and fearlessness through camping, hunting, and fishing expeditions.[36] The wilderness was dangerous enough to prove men's masculinity while remaining far safer than battlefields.

White urban elites also infused elitist ideology in the conservation movement by erecting a comprehensive set of new laws governing the use of the environment. They changed hunting rules to legitimize aristocratic sporting ethics which emphasize a fair chase, demonstration of expertise, humane killing, minimal harvesting, and providing a chance for the game animal to escape, none of which resonated with the hunting practice of rural working-class Americans, Indigenous peoples, and African Americans.[37] Elite conservationists further criminalized subsistence activities of rural Americans and Indigenous peoples by attributing the illegal acts to moral corruption and criminal instinct, although in reality they were the ones who "invented" new crimes.[38]

The leading conservationists such as Madison Grant, William Temple Hornaday, Henry Fairfield Osborn, and Theodore Roosevelt all held strong elitist, racist, eugenicist, and sexist beliefs.[39] They were all wealthy, highly educated, and closely tied with one another via elite social circles, wielding significant cultural and intellectual influence over the rest of the nation. Madison Grant, for example, was born into a privileged family in New York City, attended Yale University, and later received a law degree from Columbia Law School. He made tireless efforts to create Denali, Olympic, Everglades, and Glacier national parks, yet his effort for creating national parks, and for nature conservation in general, dovetailed with his desire for preserving the White race. In his book, *The Passing of the Great Race*, published in 1916, Grant explicated his racist and eugenicist philosophy and argued that the Nordic or White race, which developed in rough forests and cold climates in northern Europe, was physically, intellectually, and morally superior to any other races.[40]

Although the book is riddled with deductive arguments lacking clear scientific evidence, it garnered significant interest within American scientific communities and attracted a wide international readership.[41] One of the most inspired groups was the Nazi regime in Germany. The book's eugenic arguments nicely overlapped with the Nazi party's political propaganda, providing a perfect justification for the Nazis to establish sterilization and Nuremberg laws in Germany.[42] Moreover, Adolf Hitler wrote a letter of appreciation to Grant and acknowledged that the book was "my Bible."[43] His autobiographic *Mein Kampf*, published in 1925, exhibits explicit similarities to *The Passing*.[44]

One of three reviewers of Grant's book manuscript was Henry Fairfield Osborn, a leading evolutionary biologist who was ranked the second most celebrated scientist in the nation (Albert Einstein being the first).[45] Osborn was the eldest son of railroad tycoon William Henry Osborn and became a biology and zoology professor at Columbia University. He also served as co-secretary for the New York Zoological Society (NYZS) that Grant established, arguably the most prominent preservation organization of its era.[46] Not only did Osborn provide suggestions for the manuscript, but he also wrote the preface of the book, commending that Grant's eugenic theory compelled readers to "recognize the superior force and stability of heredity, as being more enduring and potent than environment" and claimed that the "conservation of that race [the Nordic race] which has given us the true spirit of Americanism, is not a matter either of racial pride or of racial prejudice; it is a matter of love of country."[47]

William Temple Hornaday served as the director of the NYZS. He was a prominent naturalist and also served as the chief taxidermist of the U.S. National Museum (later the Smithsonian National Museum of Natural History), director of the New York Zoological Park (later the Bronx Zoo),

68 *Violent and Verdant*

and the president of the American Bison Society. Perhaps few people in U.S. history played a greater role than Hornaday in protecting vanishing wild animals, especially bison, yet there was something else that he tried very hard to protect: the White race in America. Like Grant and Osborn, Hornaday believed in White supremacy and supported immigration restrictions to maintain the United States as a White nation. He venerated elite sport hunting and falsely believed that the marketing hunting conducted by Indigenous peoples, Mexicans, Blacks, the working-class, and immigrants was the main reason for the decline of bison and other wildlife in America.[48] The following quote from Hornaday's book, *Our Vanishing Wild Life*, for which Osborn wrote the foreword, tellingly captures his disdain toward non-White, working-class immigrants as well as his anxiety over attenuating White masculinity:

> Italians are pouring into America in a steady stream. They are strong, prolific, persistent and of tireless energy. New York City now contains 340,000 of them. They work while the native Americans [White Americans] sleep. Wherever they settle, their tendency is to root out the native American [White Americans] and take his place and his income. Toward wild life the Italian laborer is a human mongoose. Give him power to act, and he will quickly exterminate every wild thing that wears feathers or hair. To our songbirds he is literally a "pestilence that walketh at noonday."[49]

Among the most influential conservationists in the 19th century was Theodore Roosevelt, the 26th president of the United States. Born into a wealthy Dutch family in New York as a frail and sickly asthmatic boy, Roosevelt was introduced to outdoor activities at an early age and became an outdoor enthusiast and avid sport hunter.[50] Roosevelt is widely celebrated for his profound and lasting impact on the creation of national parks. During his presidency from 1901 to 1909, he signed legislation establishing five new national parks and the Antiquities Act of 1906, which gives U.S. presidents the authority to create national monuments from federal lands to protect significant cultural, historic, and scientific features.[51] Roosevelt used the Act to create 18 national monuments and various parks and forests, and it has been used more than 150 times by subsequent presidents.[52] Because of his numerous contributions to national parks, Roosevelt is currently commemorated at five units of the National Park System (e.g., Theodore Roosevelt National Park in North Dakota) and honored on the Mount Rushmore National Memorial in South Dakota—a symbol of American nationalism and patriotism.[53]

Despite his extraordinary work as a conservationist and national park advocate, Roosevelt is also notorious for his racist, eugenicist, and sexist character. Like Grant, Roosevelt believed that modernization had attenuated the tough character that the Nordic or so called old-stock Americans had developed through their struggle with wild nature.[54] He was obsessed with manliness and "almost fanatically concerned with [White] race preservation" and "feared that the white race would become soft and allow itself to be pushed out of first place."[55] Roosevelt considered Indigenous peoples as savages who needed to be exterminated for the nation's racial purification and African Americans as an inherently inferior race who were leaving "an indelible black mark on the white nation."[56] Thus, Roosevelt equated the degeneration of the White race with disappearing wildlife, and it was his racially charged nationalism that conceived of the preservation of wilderness, such as creating national parks, as a means to maintain White supremacy in the U.S.

Thus, for the White elite conservation leaders, creating national parks was more than a work of personal attachment to nature or protecting natural resources for the nation's economy and recreation. Rather, it was a *eugenic project* designed to protect the White race, manliness, and class nobility. According to Miles Powell, these influential conservationists expected policymakers to preserve the nation's wilderness to serve as "an evolutionary gymnasium for white Americans."[57] To them, overexploitation and destruction of the natural environment meant losing a rare opportunity to preserve White male hegemony in the U.S. It means that White elite conservation leaders nurtured both the idea and the reality of America's great outdoors as a space exclusively for the prosperity and benefit of the White race.

American Imperialism, Conservation for Profits, and Yellowstone National Park

Yellowstone holds a significant place in the history of U.S. national parks and the American conservation movement, yet similar to other early public parks, its past is ripe with violence and oppression toward vulnerable and marginalized groups. Archeological evidence indicates that the human history of the Yellowstone region goes back nearly 11,000 years, and it was a popular hunting, fishing, and camping site for multiple Indigenous groups, such as the Shoshone, Crow, Salish, Bannock, Nez Perce, Blackfeet, and Sheep Eaters.[58] However, European countries such as France, England, and Spain completely dismissed the Indigenous peoples' long history on the land and fought among themselves for its ownership, resulting in 14 different "adjustments, sales, and conquests" by 1824.[59] This land, which Euro-Americans ignorantly referred to as "natural" or "wilderness" was in fact meticulously cared for by Indigenous peoples, who shaped it through seasonal migration, prescribed fire, and herding game animals.[60]

The first Euro-American who traversed the present-day Yellowstone National Park (YNP) is a subject of much debate. In the late 18th century, many Indigenous peoples already traded with American trappers who encroached on the Yellowstone rivers. Thus, some European, American, and Canadian trappers probably ventured into the Yellowstone region during the 17th century prior to the major expeditions (or invasions) funded by the U.S. government such as the Folsom Expedition in 1869 and the Washburn Expedition in 1870.[61] However, John Colter, a trapper and fur trader who joined the Lewis and Clark Expedition, is often known as the first White American on record to penetrate the Yellowstone country.[62] In August 1806, near the end of the Lewis and Clark expedition, Colter desired to remain in the West to trade fur with Indigenous peoples and requested, and then was granted, an honorable discharge. In the following year, Colter explored today's YNP area for trapping and trading.[63]

Many other trappers and explorers wandered in the Yellowstone country after Colter. Warren Angus Ferris, a clerk of the American Fur Company, traveled to the great geysers of the Firehole River basins in 1833. Osborne Russell also went into the Yellowstone region multiple times from 1835 to 1839 and left some of the most comprehensive early accounts of its wilderness. James "Jim" Bridger, who joined the 1822 Missouri River expedition organized by General William H. Ashley and Major Andrew Henry, became a highly knowledgeable and accomplished trapper in the Yellowstone region. Once fur trading as an organized business ended in the northern Rocky Mountains in the 1840s, Bridger served as a guide of the American West for new settlers, notables such as Sir William Drummond Stewart, and several army expeditions.[64]

Discovery of gold along the Snake River in the 1860s further fueled the migration of many miners and prospectors to the region.[65] Among them was John Bozeman, a Georgian who moved to Colorado and then Montana. Recognizing a need for a more direct overland route to the West, Bozeman and John Jacobs pioneered the Bozeman Trail which ranged from Fort Laramie, Wyoming to Virginia City, Montana and it became the most popular route to the Northwest in the 1860s. Bozeman also believed in the agricultural potential of the Gallatin Valley and played a major role in the establishment of the town of Bozeman, later the city of Bozeman, in Montana.[66]

Although generations of Americans have celebrated and glorified adventurous stories of these early explorers of Yellowstone, it is important to note that they are one-sided, telling only the White American perspective. Distinguished environmental historian William Cronon pointed out that by making ordinary people into heroes and Indigenous peoples the foil for the story of progress and adventure, the frontier plot makes the American conquest against the Indigenous seem "natural, commonsensical, inevitable."[67] Paul Schullery also keenly reminded us that the historical reality is far more complicated and multifaceted. Those explorers were trappers hired by fur trading companies who were sent or driven out West for profit making. Moreover, their considerable geographical knowledge helped open new routes for other trappers, miners, and settlers, contributing to the long and painful path of displacement, genocide, and forced assimilation of Indigenous peoples.[68] John Bozeman, for instance, has been widely celebrated as a pathfinder, frontiersman, and visionary, yet he blazed the new migration route by cutting through the heart of Crow Country as defined by the Fort Laramie Treaty of 1851. During the peace commission's councils in 1867, both the Crow and Sioux demanded an immediate abandonment of the trail, because it only worsened the American encroachment into the Indigenous lands.[69] Hence, for Indigenous peoples, those "explorers" were nothing but the intruders or invaders of their homelands whom they must fight against.

Visited by many traders, miners, explorers, and tourists, Yellowstone gradually gained national acclaim as America's most prominent natural wonderland. Soon, the capitalist mindset was disseminated within the region by frontier entrepreneurs and opportunists. They not only built a toll bridge, hotels, and bathhouses but also organized a regular passenger service between Bozeman and Mammoth Hot Spring.[70] Individuals with respected social statuses started to conceive of Yellowstone as an endangered place that should be reserved for public use rather than private ownership. For example, Governor of Montana Territory Thomas F. Meagher (1865) and the leader of the Folsom Expedition David E. Folsom (1869) suggested that Yellowstone needed to be turned into a public park.[71]

Ironically, a decisive movement to make Yellowstone a public park was made by individuals with strong commercial interests, namely those in the railroad business. When Ferdinand V. Hayden, a medical doctor and the head of the U.S. Geological and Geographical Survey of the Territories, came back from his first scientific exploration of Yellowstone in October 1871, he found on his desk a letter sent by A.B. Nettleton, a representative of Jay Cooke & Company and Northern Pacific Railroad. The letter states:

> Dear Doctor:
> Judge Kelley has made a suggestion which strikes me as being an excellent one, viz.: Let Congress pass a bill reserving the Great Geyser Basin as a public park forever – just as it has reserved that far inferior wonder the Yosemite valley and big trees. If you approve this would such a recommendation be appropriate in your official report?[72]

The "Judge Kelley" mentioned in the letter was William D. Kelley, a Philadelphia jurist and ardent supporter of railroad expansion who was heavily involved in the affairs of Jay Cooke & Company, a major financier of the Northern Pacific Railroad. Kelley preferred to advance his suggestion through Nettleton rather than directly in Congress, probably due to his close association with the railroad industry. Jay Cooke was another strong supporter of making Yellowstone a national park, because it would lead to more business expansion of the Northern Pacific.[73]

Hayden responded to the letter positively because he, too, had developed intimate relationships with railroad companies since his early career stage as a geological surveyor. Union Pacific Railroad used to provide free passes for Hayden's explorations, because the findings from the explorations would help the company build new routes and entice more travelers.[74] Hayden even surveyed a certain Yellowstone area "at the instigation of J. Cooke & Co." because the Northern Pacific Railroad was interested in running a branch road and connecting it with the Central Pacific.[75] Making Yellowstone a national park would only benefit him and further solidify his relationship with the Northern Pacific.

Hayden eagerly joined the ranks of the petitioners and vigorously lobbied Congress to pass the park bill which was introduced in both Houses of Congress in 1871. The bill stated that, similar to Yosemite Valley and the Mariposa Redwood Grove, Yellowstone was "dedicated and set apart as a public park or pleasuring ground for the benefit and enjoyment of the people."[76] Hayden put together a major exhibit in the Capitol rotunda displaying geological specimens, sketches, and photographs from his Yellowstone expedition. He also served as a principal source of information on Yellowstone and was repeatedly cited on the Senate floor, certainly by all of the bill's proponents. On March 1st, 1872, President Grant signed the Yellowstone Act.[77]

Therefore, even though many Americans believe YNP represents wilderness protection from commercial development and private ownership, such an idea is an enduring hoax. In fact, capitalist development started to encroach on Yellowstone even before it became a national park, and railroad companies' avarice was a major driving force in making it the first national park in the U.S. Furthermore, commercial greed continued to make its way into Yellowstone after it became a national park. The newly established park was riddled with profit extraction by timber thieves, poachers, miners, and real estate speculators.[78] Railroad companies lobbied Congress, built new rail lines, and actively promoted Yellowstone as one of the most impressive travel destinations in the U.S. Significantly, the Department of the Interior also contributed to the commercialization of Yellowstone. In the 1880s, the federal agency leased parcels of parkland to private businesses that were financially backed by the Northern Pacific to provide visitor services such as lodging, food, transportation, and entertainment. By the time the NPS was created in 1916, concessioners were firmly entrenched in Yellowstone and the park was already a site of "some of the most intensive commercial activity in the American West."[79]

Military campaigns against Indigenous peoples are another main theme of the early stage of YNP management. In 1877, the Nez Perce War erupted in Northwestern United States.[80] Nez Perce people were pushed eastward by General Nelson A. Miles and his 2,000 soldiers. About 600 of the Nez Perce entered YNP, attacked several tourists, and took them captive. The outbreak of the Nez Perce War, along with the U.S. government's failure to meet treaty obligations, chronic food shortage, and incessant pressure on Indigenous lands by White settlers, all contributed to another acute conflict in the following year, the Bannock War in 1878. Similar to the Nez Perce, the Bannock were chased by the U.S. Army, so they decided to escape to Canada, entering YNP through the Bannock Trail. There, the Bannock raided horses, stole cattle from a ranch, and frightened tourists. Eventually, the Bannock bands were defeated by the army of Colonel Miles and Lieutenant Hoel Bishop.[81]

No doubt park officials were concerned with these "Indian troubles" and increasingly viewed Indigenous peoples as a threat to the park. During the Bannock War, Philetus Norris, the second superintendent of YNP, built the first park headquarters, a heavily fortified blockhouse, at the top of a hill at Mammoth Hot Spring, believing that it could function as the "best defensive point against Indians."[82] He also called on the Army to set up a small military post on the park's western boundary to prevent Indigenous peoples in the Fort Hall and Lemhi reservations from entering the park. Yet, during the 1880s and 1890s, Indigenous peoples continued to travel across the park boundaries, hunted and fished in the park, and used prescribed fire to maintain their hunting areas and campsites. Even though they were simply exercising the treaty rights, these activities were viewed as an abuse of natural resources and certainly not what tourists would expect from the newly established nation's wilderness wonderland that had to be pure, empty, and untouched by any civilization.[83]

Park officials and local residents gradually placed more restrictions on Indigenous activities within and beyond the park and *criminalized* their traditional hunting practices as "love of game-butchery" which was "so injurious to the park" and "wasteful and improvident."[84] Interestingly, when park managers and local residents encountered illegal hunting from White settlers, they lumped White poachers with Indigenous peoples and defined the two groups as a uniformly dangerous group. Although Indigenous groups resisted and fought for their hunting rights in YNP that were guaranteed by the Fort Bridger Treaty in 1868, the U.S. Supreme Court decision *Ward v. Race Horse* in 1896 reversed the agreement and nullified their hunting rights, allowing local officials to arrest any Indigenous peoples who ventured onto public lands, including YNP, during closed hunting seasons. Eventually, Yellowstone became "the non-Indian Wilderness" that the majority of parks officials and tourists always expected it to be.[85]

In summary, the early history of Yellowstone exemplifies the foundation of U.S. national parks marked by colonial and capitalist invasions against Indigenous peoples, as well as racist and elitist ideologies of White conservation leaders and park officials. That is, when Euro-Americans started to encroach on the Indigenous lands of today's YNP, they forced fraudulent land treaties to take away the livelihood of Indigenous groups, forced them to accept American ways of life, pushed them onto reservations, and criminalized their hunting and fishing practices as a barbarous attack on wilderness.[86] Once YNP was created, two sharply contrasting yet equally oppressive schemes against Indigenous peoples emerged. First, Indigenous cultures and civilizations were *expunged* from the parks, because the newly established nation's natural majesty should not be tainted by any human footage. This also helped Americans effectively obscure the ethnocide they committed against Indigenous peoples and justify their land ownership. Even though Americans treated Indigenous peoples as uncivilized and animal-like beings, ironically, they expected the latter should not exist in the wilderness.

74   *Violent and Verdant*

Oppression also took another form: Indigenous heritages were *explicitly visualized* for tourism marketing. As a marketing campaign, for instance, the Great Northern Railway not only featured photographs and stories about the Blackfeet in popular magazines and newspapers but also brought them to major U.S. cities to set up tepee camps on the roofs of downtown buildings.[87] This is no surprise given that the motions to create both YNP and Yosemite were made by a group of wealthy and influential individuals who were eager to gain profits from converting wilderness into popular tourism destinations. Their greed conveniently dovetailed with their desire to preserve natural beauty. The idea that national parks were created in order to protect vanishing American wilderness from rapacious private interests is indeed an enduring hoax.

Displacement, Tourism Development, and Great Smoky Mountains and Shenandoah National Parks

On May 22, 1926, more than a half-century after the creation of the first national park, President Calvin Coolidge signed a bill establishing Great Smoky Mountains National Park (GSMNP) and Shenandoah National Park (SNP). This was exciting news for many people who wanted national parks in the Eastern United States. Even though the number of national parks had grown to more than a dozen since Yellowstone, all of those parks were located west of the Mississippi River, except Lafayette (now Acadia) National Park in Maine. This uneven distribution of national parks invited Eastern policymakers' criticism that national parks were not really "national" and should be managed by each state.[88]

Stephen Mather, a millionaire businessman who became the first director of NPS in 1917, was well aware of the criticism and convinced Interior Secretary Hubert Work to form a committee investigating the creation of a national park in the Southern Appalachians.[89]

Similar to other public parks, the creation of GSMNP and SNP was galvanized by the avarice and conservation interests of rich and influential civic leaders and businessmen. In Virginia, local businessmen formed the Northern Virginia National Park Association and the Shenandoah Valley, Inc. to bring a national park to the Appalachians.[90] George Freeman Pollock, one of the key players in the park movement and the owner of the Skyland Resort in the Blue Ridge Mountains, hosted influential policymakers and congressmen at his resort and touted the need for a national park near Eastern cities. As the owner of more than 5,000 acres of the central area of what is now SNP, Pollock had strong financial motives.[91] In Tennessee, Willis Perkins Davis, the president of Knoxville Iron Company and a board member of the Knoxville Automobile Club, and his wife Ann Davis, the third woman ever elected to the Tennessee House of Representatives, helped found the Great Smoky Mountains Conservation Association, which aimed to establish a national park in the Smokies.[92] In North Carolina, wealthy urban residents were ardent supporters of the park movement. The Appalachian National Park Association, a multi-state organization, was established in Asheville in 1899. Asheville park boosters also established Great Smoky Mountains, Inc. in 1925.[93]

Yet, park advocates were also up against the formidable task of securing the lands for creating the two parks. Although the passage of the 1926 bill was thrilling news for park boosters, the proposed park lands were already occupied by mountain residents and lumber companies and the bill stipulated that those lands needed to be purchased through funds raised by state governments and private donations rather than federal funds. It meant that each adjacent state was responsible for purchasing and removing all the houses, farms, orchards, and lumber companies in the park boundaries and then transferring the lands to the federal government.[94]

In Virginia, two new organizations were at the forefront of the removal process: the Shenandoah National Park Association, a private group of local elites focused on the fundraising drive, and the Commission on Conservation and Development (CCD), a state agency handling the legal issues involved in acquiring the land. William E. Carson, the president of the CCD, successfully persuaded Hubert Work, the Secretary of the Interior, and other NPS officials to reduce the park boundary to alleviate the total cost of the land purchase. Carson also proposed one blanket condemnation law to acquire the parkland. Fearing that real estate transactions with individual residents could lead to numerous jury trials and appeals, which would substantially delay the whole process, Carson proposed to the General Assembly to condemn all the land in the park area through one blanket condemnation law, enabling the state to purchase the required lands through eminent domain. Notably, this idea came from A.C. Carson, William's brother, who became familiar with condemnation laws while he served as a judge of the Philippines Supreme Court from 1904 to 1920. William Carson hired his brother for legal advice without authorization from the CCD or the Governor.[95]

The situation in Tennessee and North Carolina was not so different. In April 1927, a bill was passed in the Tennessee General Assembly which appropriated $1.5 million for purchasing the parkland and granted the Tennessee Great Smoky Mountains Park Commission the power to seize homes within the proposed park boundaries by rights of eminent domain. North Carolina followed suit with an 11-member park commission and a $2 million appropriation. Fundraising campaigns were launched, and the Rockefeller Foundation donated $5 million. Having secured enough capital, the state governments proceeded with the land purchase plan and were ready to enforce eminent domain.[96]

The ways that mountain people were treated and displaced by the state and park officials exhibit striking similarities to the fate of the Indigenous peoples in Yellowstone. First, the displacement processes were deceptive as those with power preyed on vulnerable groups and frequently betrayed trust. For instance, although Tennessee Governor Austin Peay, Senator Lawrence

Tyson, and the Park Commission repeatedly assured that the park bill would not take away Smoky residents' lands, their promises eventually turned out to be "blatant deceit." For Shenandoah, the NPS director Arno Cammerer announced in February 1924 that the federal government would not accept any parklands until all inhabitants had left the area, the announcement stemming from problems the federal government previously encountered with the people left in Great Smoky. Virginia officials were caught off-guard because they underestimated the timing and scale of the removal and soon were bombarded by many "poignant or belligerent" letters from park residents. Similar to how Indigenous people were dispossessed of their land under the U.S. government's fraudulent land treaties and broken promises, many Appalachian mountaineers felt that they were robbed and had no choice but to vacate their lands.[97]

Second, consistent with how things unfolded in Yellowstone, the displacement process in the Appalachian entailed two opposite yet equally oppressive schemes for mountain residents. On one hand, park advocates attempted to erase the culture of the residents, because the new national parks had to represent pristine natural environment containing no human footprint. Accordingly, after the residents left, NPS officials and CCC units burned down or removed the empty houses, community infrastructure, farms, and orchards in order to eradicate the evidence of mountain culture in GSMNP and SNP.[98] *Stereotyping* made the erasure easier. Most park advocates labeled mountain residents as poor, ignorant, uncivilized, promiscuous, and immoral, all negative and false characterizations helpful for instigating the park displacement. On the other hand, park advocates saw from the beginning of the park movement that the local folk culture was something they could capitalize on. Smoky residents were described as "contemporary ancestors" and old people maintaining old-fashioned lifestyles, an enticing description for curious tourists. When selecting local residents and buildings that would remain on the parklands, NPS officials preferred people who could exhibit mountain culture as well as buildings with a historic appearance to attract tourists. Just like how Indigenous peoples and their culture were erased yet also commercialized in Yellowstone, park advocates made mountain peoples either visible or invisible depending on their needs.[99]

Finally, the removal of mountain residents involved violent displacement. Although the majority of mountaineers eventually vacated their homes and properties, many of them were deeply attached to the area and did not wish to leave. Moreover, the Great Depression and plummeting property values made the relocation even more challenging for the residents. Some of them chose to, or had no choice but to, ignore eviction orders and eventually met with forced removal from local law enforcement, while others fiercely fought back to keep the lands that their families had cultivated for multiple generations.[100] For example, Robert H. Via, the owner of a 150-acre orchard in Virginia, sued the state government on the grounds that the condemnation laws violated his 14th Amendment rights, and took the case all the way up to the Supreme Court.[101] Lewis Willis not only led a group of frustrated landowners and formed the Landowners' Protective Association in 1929, but also sent a letter to President Hoover, stating that, "We are unwilling to part with our homes to help a small part of our population to get their hands into tourists' pockets."[102] When White Americans invaded Yellowstone and Yosemite, many Indigenous peoples bravely fought back to protect their livelihood, family, and friends. So did the Appalachian people.

However, the Appalachian people eventually followed a similar fate of Indigenous peoples in Yellowstone and Yosemite. An estimate showed that 5,665 people left their homes for the creation of GSMNP and 385 were tenant farmers who received nothing from either the state or the federal government for relocation.[103] In SNP, the removal order affected approximately 500 to 600 families or 3,000 to 4,000 people. By the time President Franklin Roosevelt attended the SNP dedication ceremony on July 3, 1936, some mountain residents still lived in the park because they could not secure their new homes due to a lack of means and federal support.[104]

In addition to the striking similarity between the Indian removal in YNP and the displacement of mountain residents in GSMNP and SNP, there exists another distinctive yet often forgotten connection between the national parks in the West and the East. Judge A.C. Carson who was instrumental in implementing the one blanket condemnation law in SNP, drew inspiration from legal cases in the Philippines, a country the United States annexed through the Philippine-American War in 1899. Notably, 26 of the 30 U.S. Generals in the Philippines had previously been involved in Indian Wars in the homeland, and among them, Nelson A. Miles, who pushed Nez Perce people to YNP during the Nez Perce War, was put in general command of the U.S. Army in the Philippines.[105] In this history, the tale of the eastern and western national parks uniquely converges, illustrating the lasting impact of American imperialism and colonialism in both domestic and international landscapes.

U.S. National Parks: Eternal Zero-Sum Game?

> *The problem of today is simply that the parks are being loved to death.*
> Conrad Wirth, 6th Director of National Park Service, January 27, 1956[106]

> *The national parks are the best idea we ever had. Absolutely American, absolutely democratic, they reflect us at our best rather than our worst.*
> Wallace Stegner, Pulitzer Prize-winning novelist[107]

The above statements from Conrad Wirth and Wallace Stegner have been some of the most widely cited praises of U.S. national parks. Wirth made the infamous "loved to death" speech to convince President Dwight D. Eisenhower and the cabinet to support the Mission 66 project, a 10-year infrastructure improvement plan for national parks. With his succinct and powerful statement, backed by statistics showing the staggering increase in the number of national park visitors since the 1910s, Wirth successfully garnered political support for Mission 66.

But were national parks really loved to death? If so, *by whom*? The answer to this question could be found in *A Survey of the Public Concerning the National Parks*, a study report published two years after Wirth's infamous speech. It shows that out of a 1,754 U.S. adult sample, White Americans constituted 95% of the respondents who visited a national park in the last five years while the rest of 5% was "Colored" Americans. Among those park visitors, 33% had a college education and 20% had an annual family income of $7,000 and over (the highest income category in the survey). Among the Americans who never visited a national park, individuals with the same education and income levels comprised only 9%, respectively.[108] These visitor statistics indicate that there was a big caveat in Wirth's statement: National parks were loved to death mainly by a specific segment of Americans who were well-educated, White, and upper-class.

The racial and ethnic disparity documented by the report is hardly surprising, given that the NPS had a "conscious, but unpublicized policy of discouraging visits by African Americans" and segregated facilities were rarely provided until the late 1940s.[109] In fact, park rangers used various methods to discourage African Americans' access to parks and park concessionaires also denied service to African Americans or offered limited segregated facilities.[110] Although the NPS officially banned racial segregation in national parks in 1948, only a handful of national parks had segregated park facilities for African Americans. Furthermore, most parks followed the "local custom," and the directors of individual park units and local authorities resisted the racial integration order from the NPS headquarters and the federal government in Washington, D.C.[111]

More troubling yet is that since the time of Wirth, there have been little to no changes in the demographic profile of national park visitors. The three NPS reports published in 2000, 2008–09, and 2018 have commonly documented that national parks were visited disproportionally by affluent and highly educated White Americans, while people of color and low-income groups constituted a small portion of the total visitor.[112]

With all the above information, compounded by the parks' troubling history of ethnic cleansing against Indigenous peoples and displacement of mountain residents, I cannot stop questioning Wallace Stegner's commendation of national parks: Exactly *what aspects* of national parks are "the best ideas" of Americans? Is ethnic cleansing against Indigenous peoples and violent displacement of mountain people "absolutely democratic"? Is economic exploitation and criminalization of those people really a reflection of the country's "best" rather than the "worst"?

To be fair, there is no doubt that U.S. national parks contribute to the environmental protection and public recreation of the country. After all, as articulated in the Yellowstone Act in 1872 and the National Park Service Organic Act in 1916, those benefits are what national parks are supposed to provide to all Americans.

But, I must ask, conservation and public recreation *at what cost*? As illustrated in this chapter, what lies at the very foundation of U.S. national parks are American imperialism and colonialism, capitalist exploitation, and the racist and eugenic ideology of some of the most affluent and powerful individuals in this country. Who, then, would be able to say definitively that national parks' conservation and recreation benefits outweigh the lives and wellbeing of those massacred Indigenous peoples and displaced mountain people? How do we know for sure that national parks are more important than the lingering generational suffering of those people? Moreover, how could parks established mainly through the commercial and financial interests of the rich and the powerful be viewed as a democratic space? If the genocide and displacement are justified in the name of nature conservation and public recreation, it seems the only plausible explanation for U.S. national parks is that they represent extreme consequentialism—the idea that the end justifies the means. So is that what American conservation is all about or how we want to teach the next generations about conservation?

Notes

1 "Franklin D. Roosevelt: Radio Address from Two Medicine Chalet, Glacier National Park," August 5, 1934, https://www.presidency.ucsb.edu/node/208548.
2 Eean Grimshaw, "Native America Speaks: Blackfeet Communication and Culture in Glacier National Park" (Ph.D. University of Massachusetts, Amherst, 2022), 144.
3 J.M. Burns, *Roosevelt: The Lion and the Fox (1882–1940)* (Harcourt Brace Jovanovich, 1984), 24.
4 John C. Paige, *The Civilian Conservation Corps and the National Park Service, 1933-1942: An Administrative History* (National Park Service, US Department of the Interior, 1985).
5 Lary M. Dilsaver, *America's national park system: The critical documents* (Rowman & Littlefield, 2016), 1; Wallace Stegner, *Marking the Sparrow's Fall: Wallace Stegner's American West* (Henry Holt & Co, 1998), 135.
6 For the quote, see Denis Cosgrove, "Habitable Earth: Wilderness, Empire, and Race in America," in *Wild Ideas*, ed. D. Rothenberg (University of Minnesota Press, 1995), 36; Philip Burnham, *Indian Country, God's Country: Native Americans and the National Parks* (Island Press, 2000); Jason Byrne and Jennifer Wolch, "Nature, race, and parks: past research and future directions for geographic research," *Progress in Human Geography* 33, no. 6 (2009); Isaac Kantor, "Ethnic cleansing and America's creation of national parks," *Public Land & Resources Law Review* 28 (2007); Robert H. Keller and Michael F. Turek, *American Indians and National Parks* (University of Arizona Press, 1998); Mark David Spence, *Dispossessing the Wilderness: Indian Removal and the Making of the National Parks* (Oxford University Press, 1999).
7 G. Catlin, *Letters and Notes on the Manners, Customs, and Condition of the North American Indian. Volume 1* (Egyptian Hall, 1841), 262.
8 Alfred Runte, *National Parks: The American Experience* (University of Nebraska Press, 1997), 41.
9 Miles A. Powell, *Vanishing America: Species Extinction, Racial Peril, and the Origins of Conservation* (Harvard University Press, 2016).
10 Roderick Frazier Nash, *Wilderness and the American mind* (Yale University Press, 2014); Dorceta E. Taylor, *The Rise of the American Conservation Movement: Power, Privilege, and Environmental Protection* (Duke University Press, 2016), 291–93.
11 Aubrey L. Haines, *The Yellowstone Story: A History of Our First National Park*, vol. 1 (Yellowstone National Park, Wyoming: Yellowstone Library and Museum Association, 1996), 130, 56; Paul Schullery and Lee H. Whittlesey, *Myth and History in the Creation of Yellowstone National Park* (University of Nebraska Press, 2003); Lee H. Whittlesey, "Loss of a Sacred Shrine: How the National Park Service Anguished over Yellowstone's Campfire Myth, 1960-1980," *The George Wright Forum* 27, no. 1 (2010).
12 Haines, *The Yellowstone Story*, 1, 103.
13 "The past is where the fun is," n.d., https://www.hotsprings.org/explore/history/#:~:text=The%20hot%20springs%20were%20such,National%20Park%20by%2040%20years; Runte, *National Parks*, 26.
14 Alfred Runte, *Yosemite: The Embattled Wilderness* (University of Nebraska Press, 1990), 26; Haines, *The Yellowstone Story*, 1, 163.

15 Louis Convers Cramton, *Early History of Yellowstone National Park and Its Relation to National Park Policies* (US Government Printing Office, 1932).
16 "Birth of a National Park," U.S. Department of the Interior, 2020, accessed December 30 2023, https://www.nps.gov/yell/learn/historyculture/yellowstoneestablishment.htm.
17 Dilsaver, *America's National Park System*, Chapter 1.
18 The U.S. government and Army also killed bison to push Indigenous peoples out of their territories and make them starved or economically subjugated. This was because Indigenous peoples depended on bison for food, clothes, shelter, and tools. See Burnham, *Indian Country, God's Country*; Carolyn Merchant, *American Environmental History: An Introduction* (Columbia University Press, 2007), 20.
19 M. Scott Taylor, "Buffalo hunt: International trade and the virtual extinction of the North American bison," *American Economic Review* 101, no. 7 (2011).
20 Powell, *Vanishing America*, 51.
21 Hank Johnston, "Yosemite: The first National Park," *Yosemite Association* 61, no. 3 (1999): 2.
22 Alfred Runte, "The national park idea: origins and paradox of the American experience," *Journal of Forest History* 21, no. 2 (1977): 66.
23 Runte, "The national park idea," 65; Runte, *National Parks*, 32.
24 Nash, *Wilderness and the American Mind*, Chapter 4; Runte, *National Parks*, 7–8.
25 Runte, "The national park idea," 68. It is noteworthy that Paul Schullery points out that none of the early explorers Runte quoted, such as Charles Cook, Nathaniel Langford, and Gustavus Doane, actually juxtaposed Yellowstone with European landscapes. Schullery argued that Runte's cultural anxiety or insecurity argument is "entirely conjectural" in the case of Yellowstone. See Paul Schullery, *Searching for Yellowstone: Ecology and Wonder in the Last Wilderness* (Montana Historical Society, 2004), 63.
26 Dorceta E. Taylor, *The Environment and the People in American Cities, 1600s–1900s: Disorder, Inequality, and Social Change* (Duke University Press, 2009).
27 Nash, *Wilderness and the American Mind*, Chapter 3, Chapter 5; Taylor, *The Rise of the American Conservation Movement*, 58–63.
28 Nash, *Wilderness and the American Mind*, 78.
29 Nash, *Wilderness and the American Mind*, Chapter 2, 36, 41–42.
30 Nash, *Wilderness and the American Mind*, Chapter 2, 36, 41–42.
31 William Cronon, "The trouble with wilderness: or, getting back to the wrong nature," *Environmental History* 1, no. 1 (1996).
32 Roderick Nash, "The American invention of national parks," *American Quarterly* 22, no. 3 (1970): 728.
33 Taylor, *The Rise of the American Conservation Movement*, Chapter 1.
34 Powell, *Vanishing America*, 55, 104–08.
35 Taylor, *The Rise of the American Conservation Movement*, 80.
36 Taylor, *The Rise of the American Conservation Movement*, Chapter 3, 346; Powell, *Vanishing America*, 83–84.
37 Karl Jacoby, *Crimes Against Nature: Squatters, Poachers, Thieves, and the Hidden History of American Conservation* (University of California Press, 2014); Taylor, *The Rise of the American Conservation Movement*, 186.
38 Jacoby, *Crimes Against Nature*, 2.
39 Gary Gerstle, "Theodore Roosevelt and the divided character of American nationalism," *The Journal of American History* 86, no. 3 (1999); Rasul A. Mowatt, "A

People's History of Leisure Studies: The Great Race and the National Parks and U.S. Forests," *Journal of Park and Recreation Administration* 38, no. 3 (2020); Powell, *Vanishing America*.
40 Jonathan Peter Spiro, *Defending the Master Race: Conservation, Eugenics, and the Legacy of Madison Grant* (University Press of New England, 2009).
41 Spiro, *Defending the Master Race*, 161–66.
42 Spiro, *Defending the Master Race*, 365.
43 Leon Fradley Whitney, 1971, "Leon Fradley Whitney Autobiography, Page 33", American Philosophical Society. https://diglib.amphilsoc.org/islandora/object/text%3A287794
44 Spiro, *Defending the Master Race*, 357.
45 Brian Regal, *Henry Fairfield Osborn: Race and the Search for the Origins of Man* (Ashgate 2002), xii.
46 Regal, *Henry Fairfield Osborn*, xii.
47 H.F. Osborn, "Preface," in *The Passing of the Great Race* (Charles Scribner's Sons, 1916), vii–ix.
48 Powell, *Vanishing America*, 84–85, 94.
49 William Temple Hornaday, *Our Vanishing Wild Life: Its Extermination and Preservation* (Charles Scribner's Sons, 1913), 101.
50 Taylor, *The Rise of the American Conservation Movement*, 73.
51 Robert W. Righter, "Theodore Roosevelt and the National Park Systems" (October 30 2015). http://npshistory.com/publications/roosevelt/index.htm.
52 U.S. Department of the Interior, Concerning the Designation of Monuments Pursuant to the Authority Provided by the Antiquities Act (U.S. Department of the Interior, 2016).
53 Righter, "Theodore Roosevelt and the National Park Systems."
54 Thomas G. Dyer, *Theodore Roosevelt and the Idea of Race* (LSU Press, 1992).
55 George Sinkler, *The Racial Attitudes of American Presidents: From Abraham Lincoln to Theodore Roosevelt* (Doubleday & Co., 1971), 337–39.
56 Gerstle, "Theodore Roosevelt," 1285.
57 Powell, *Vanishing America*, 84.
58 Joel C. Janetski, *Indians in Yellowstone National Park* (Salt Lake City: University of Utah Press, 2002); Douglas H. MacDonald, *Before Yellowstone: Native American Archaeology in the National Park* (University of Washington Press, 2018); Peter Nabokov and Lawrence L. Loendorf, *Restoring a Presence: American Indians and Yellowstone National Park* (University of Oklahoma Press, 2004).
59 Schullery, *Searching for Yellowstone*, 32.
60 Spence, *Dispossessing the Wilderness*, 44–45.
61 Schullery, *Searching for Yellowstone*, Chapter 2.
62 Burton Harris, *John Colter: His Years in the Rockies* (University of Nebraska Press, 1993).
63 Harris, *John Colter*, 36, 54. Richard A. Bartlett, *Nature's Yellowstone* (University of Arizona Press, 1989), 97–98.
64 Haines, *The Yellowstone Story*, 1, Chapter 2; Stanley Vestal, *Jim Bridger, Mountain Man: A Biography* (University of Nebraska Press, 1946).
65 Haines, *The Yellowstone Story*, 1, 67.
66 Merrill G. Burlingame, "John M. Bozeman, Montana Trailmaker," *The Mississippi Valley Historical Review* 27, no. 4 (1941).

67 William Cronon, "A place for stories: Nature, history, and narrative," *The Journal of American History* 78, no. 4 (1992): 1352.
68 Schullery, *Searching for Yellowstone*, 35.
69 Frank Rzeczkowski, "The crow Indians and the Bozeman trail," *Montana: The Magazine of Western History* 49, no. 4 (1999).
70 Mark Daniel Barringer, *Selling Yellowstone: Capitalism and the Construction of Nature* (University Press of Kansas, 2002), 16–18.
71 Haines, *The Yellowstone Story*, 1, 90, 103.
72 Aubrey L. Haines, *Yellowstone National Park: Its Exploration and Establishment* (US National Park Service, 1974), 109.
73 Haines, *Yellowstone National Park*, 110.
74 Gerald James Cassidy, "Ferdinand V. Hayden: Federal entrepreneur of science" (Ph.D. University of Pennsylvania, 1991), 131–32.
75 Haines, *Yellowstone National Park*, 153.
76 Dilsaver, *America's National Park System*, 20.
77 Haines, *The Yellowstone Story*, 1, 166, 71–72.
78 Taylor, *The Rise of the American Conservation Movement*, 302.
79 For the quote, Barringer, *Selling Yellowstone*, 7. For the lease and commercialization, see page 6. For the railroad companies' lobbies, see page 39. See also H. Duane Hampton, *How the U.S. Cavalry Saved Our National Parks* (Indiana University Press, 1971).
80 It stemmed from a "thief" treaty in 1863 in which the U.S. government demanded the Nez Perce to give up 90% of their territories ensured by the 1855 Treaty of Walla Walla and move to a reservation in Idaho. See John K. Flanagan, "The Invalidity of the Nez Perce Treaty of 1863 and the Taking of the Wallowa Valley," *American Indian Law Review* 24, no. 1 (1999).
81 Janetski, *Indians in Yellowstone National Park*, Chapter 5, Chapter 6.
82 P. H. Conger, *Annual Report of the Superintendent of the Yellowstone National Park to the Secretary of the Interior: For the Year 1883*, US Government Printing Office (Washington D.C., 1883), 5.
83 Spence, *Dispossessing the Wilderness*, 57–60.
84 "Protect the National Parks," *Frank Leslie's Illustrated Newspaper* (New York) April 27, 1889, 182. For the third quotation, see Moses Harris, *Annual Report of the Superintendent of the Yellowstone National Park to the Secretary of the Interior: For the Year 1889*, Department of Interior (Washington DC, 1889), 15.
85 For equating White poachers and Indigenous groups, see Jacoby, *Crimes Against Nature*, 125. For *Ward v. Race Horse* and the quotation, see Spence, *Dispossessing the Wilderness*, 68.
86 Kantor, "Ethnic cleansing."; Carolyn Merchant, "Shades of darkness: Race and environmental history," *Environmental History* 8, no. 3 (2003).
87 For the cultural exploitation and erasure, see Spence, *Dispossessing the Wilderness*, 83, 130.
88 *These American Lands: Parks, Wilderness, and the Public Lands: Revised and Expanded Edition* (Island Press, 1994), 27.
89 Dennis E. Simmons, "Conservation, cooperation, and controversy: The establishment of Shenandoah National Park, 1924-1936," *The Virginia Magazine of History and Biography* (1981).
90 Simmons, "Conservation, cooperation, and controversy," 391.

84 Violent and Verdant

91 George F. Pollock, *Skyland: The Heart of the Shenandoah National Park* (Virginia Book Co., 1960).

92 Daniel Smith Pierce, "Boosters, bureaucrats, politicians and philanthropists: coalition building in the establishment of the Great Smoky Mountains National Park" (Doctoral The University of Tennessee, 1995), 27.

93 For the wealthy urban supporter, see Margaret Lynn Brown, "Captains of Tourism: Selling a National Park in the Great Smoky Mountains," *Journal of the Appalachian Studies Association* 4 (1992): 43. For the Appalachian National Park Association, see Willard Badgette Gatewood, "North Carolina's role in the establishment of the Great Smoky Mountains National Park," *The North Carolina Historical Review* 37, no. 2 (1960). For the Great Smoky Mountains, Inc, see Pierce, "Boosters, bureaucrats, politicians and philanthropists," 74.

94 Simmons, "Conservation, cooperation, and controversy," 392–93; Terence Young, "False, cheap and degraded: when history, economy and environment collided at Cades Cove, Great Smoky Mountains National Park," *Journal of Historical Geography* 32, no. 1 (2006).

95 Simmons, "Conservation, cooperation, and controversy."; John F. Horan Jr, "Will Carson and the Virginia Conservation Commission, 1926-1934," *The Virginia Magazine of History and Biography* 92, no. 4 (1984): 411.

96 For the Tennessee bill, see Durwood Dunn, *Cades Cove: The Life and Death of a Southern Appalachian Community* (The University of Tennessee Press, 1988), 246. For the North Carolina commission, see Brown, "Captains of Tourism," 44. For the Rockefeller Foundation, see Dunn, *Cades Cove*, 247.

97 For the case of Tennessee, see Dunn, *Cades Cove*, 246. For Cammerer's announcement, see Charles L. Perdue and Nancy J. Martin-Perdue, "Appalachian fables and facts: A case study of the Shenandoah National Park removals," *Appalachian Journal* 7, no. 1/2 (1979). For the case of Virginia officials, see Simmons, "Conservation, cooperation, and controversy," 401.

98 Simmons, "Conservation, cooperation, and controversy," 402; Young, "False, cheap and degraded," 175.

99 For the stereotyping, see Brown, "Captains of Tourism," 47; Perdue and Martin-Perdue, "Appalachian fables and facts: A case study of the Shenandoah National Park removals," 89. For the historic appearance, see Young, "False, cheap and degraded," 177, 80.

100 Simmons, "Conservation, cooperation, and controversy"; Perdue and Martin-Perdue, "Appalachian fables and facts: A case study of the Shenandoah National Park removals."

101 Darwin Lambert, *The Undying Past of Shenandoah National Park* (Roberts Rinehart, Inc. & Shenandoah Natural History Association, 1989), 237; Simmons, "Conservation, cooperation, and controversy," 402.

102 Lambert, *The Undying Past of Shenandoah National Park*, 231.

103 Margaret Lynn Brown, *The Wild East: A Biography of the Great Smoky Mountains* (University Press of Florida, 2000), 98.

104 Simmons, "Conservation, cooperation, and controversy," 400–03.

105 Roxanne Dunbar-Ortiz, *An Indigenous Peoples' History of the United States* (Beacon Press, 2014), 164.

106 Dilsaver, *America's National Park System*, 170.

107 Stegner, *Marking the Sparrow's Fall*, 135.

108 Audience Research Inc., *A Survey of the Public Concerning the National Parks* (1955), 38-39.
109 Terence Young, "'A Contradiction in Democratic Government': WJ Trent, Jr., and the Struggle to Desegregate National Park Campgrounds," *Environmental History* 14, no. 4 (2009): 652.
110 Susan Shumaker, "Untold stories from America's national parks," *Segregation in the National Parks* Part 1 (2009), www.pbs.org/nationalparks/untold-stories/.
111 Young, "'A Contradiction in Democratic Government'"; Susan Shumaker, "Untold stories from America's national parks," *Segregation in the National Parks* 1 (2009): 29.
112 Resource Systems Group & Wyoming Survey and Analysis Center, *National Park Service comprehensive survey of the American public: 2018 – racial and ethnic diversity of National Park System visitors and non-visitors* (National Park Service, 2019); Jerry J. Vaske and Katie M. Lyon, *Linking the 2010 census to national park visitors: Natural Resource Technical Report NPS* (National Park Service, 2014); Xiao Xiao, KangJae Jerry Lee, and Lincoln R. Larson, "Who visits U.S. national parks (and who doesn't)? A national study of perceived constraints and vacation preferences across diverse populations," *Journal of Leisure Research* 53, no. 3 (2022).

PART II

4 Systemic Park Injustice and the People's Resistance

The neighborhood is changing. I just don't think we [Latinx] are part of the change ... part of the plan. You seem to be a smart young man, so you know what the condos going up means ... who those are meant for. This trail is great, but it wasn't put here for us, it's for the people coming in.
Mila (pseudonym), Latinx of Puerto Rican[1]

I'm not sure if it's here to help us or tear us apart and push us out.
Austen Johnson, a resident of the Southside neighborhood in Atlanta[2]

I want to push back a little bit on this notion that Bridge Park is necessarily something that the community wants, even though [the director] may have had 200 meetings...that process is tainted by segments of the community that [are] pro-development, they have interest in the value of their homes, but the average working person in that area is not thinking about Bridge Park. Most people don't even really know what the project is.
Anonymous, a civil rights attorney and a resident of Anacostia[3]

Mila was a resident of Humboldt Park, a major Puerto Rican community on the West Side of Chicago. She shared her astute observation about the Bloomingdale Trail, also known as "The 606," a 2.7-mile-long greenway and pocket park series built on an abandoned rail line. Humboldt Park is located at the west end of the trail, and local property values increased by 48.2% from the groundbreaking of the trail in 2013 to 2016. The gentrification triggered by the 606 project made Humboldt Park residents vulnerable to displacement pressure.[4]

Austen Johnson was a resident of the Southside community near Atlanta, Georgia. His short and straightforward comment was about the Belt Line project, a multiphase green space development on decommissioned rail lines. Although it is one of the largest development projects in the U.S. connecting 45 neighborhoods via 22 miles of trails, parks, and streetcars, criticisms have

DOI: 10.4324/9781032707624-7

mounted that it has not included sufficient affordable housing and therefore exacerbated the class and racial divides of the city through increased property values and taxes. While Atlanta is known as the second worst city for income inequality in the U.S., an analysis revealed that the burden of increased property taxes will fall heaviest on low-income homeowners, who are mostly people of color.[5]

The anonymous civil rights attorney described the lack of fair community input during the planning process of the 11th Street Bridge Park in Washington, D.C. The project began in late 2023, with the idea of connecting the east and west sides of the Anacostia River. Neighborhoods on the east side are Anacostia and Fairlawn, predominantly African American communities with high poverty and unemployment rates. On the west side are Navy Yard and Capitol Hill, two wealthy White communities. Despite the explicit articulation of issues of equity, inclusivity, and community engagement in the park's planning, the majority of Anacostia and Fairlawn residents were not even aware of the project and some of them were fiercely against it. Community organizers and activists were also concerned about gentrification and displacement of local residents, since 70% of them were renters and home prices in the Historic Anacostia neighborhood had already soared in 2015. These distressing concerns have been sparsely covered in media outlets, which instead lauded the project with heartwarming descriptions of the economic, environmental, social, and health benefits of the $92 million project that is expected to be completed by early 2026.[6]

The history of park injustice is not a distant past, but an ongoing social reality in the U.S. As in the case of the national capital and other major cities, American public parks continue to inflict disproportional harm to historically undeserved groups such as the working-class and people of color. It is a recurring pattern of injustice that stretches all the way back to the beginning of Boston Common and Central Park and remains to the present day. Is it possible to stop this lingering park injustice that has gained so much momentum over centuries of violence and oppression?

Any serious attempt to address the question must begin with a firm grasp of how and why systemic park injustice was initiated and perpetuated. It is also important to understand that even though systemic park injustice is enduring and pervasive, many people have pushed back as I illustrated in the previous chapters. To better understand this complex historical interplay between the park injustice and resistance, it is worth conducting a more pointed analysis on the tactics used by each side. Accordingly, this chapter first provides a more formal conceptualization of systemic park injustice, outlining 14 specific strategies that the White ruling class has employed to keep public parks for the rich and powerful. The second section of the chapter summarizes 13 counterstrategies that have been developed and utilized by contemporary park practitioners, activists, and researchers in order to neutralize systemic park injustice.

Systemic Park Injustice and Its Playbook

Systemic park injustice denotes the sociohistorical pattern that people with means and power use public parks to primarily benefit themselves while exploiting and disenfranchising people with limited resources and power. As illustrated in previous chapters, this type of violence and oppression against vulnerable and marginalized groups has been recurring and widespread across different times and locations. In this historical dynamic between the oppressors and the oppressed, the former has employed a series of social, cultural, and legal practices to monopolize the benefits of public parks while limiting the latter's access to them. Below, I summarize 14 of those discriminatory practices that have lingered in the history of American public parks. These strategies have collectively contributed to the formation of systemic park injustice, a durable material reality that perpetuates or exacerbates the power imbalance and social polarization between White elites and minoritized communities.

1. Conceptualization and Legitimization

The pioneers of American public parks, as well as the leaders of the American conservation movement, were predominantly White elite males who had significant wealth, power, and social recognition. Through their professional activities, social networking, writings, and speeches, these elites first defined what public parks meant and arbitrarily legitimized park use and outdoor recreation behaviors that were imbued with patriarchal and middle- and upper-class sensibilities. For example, Frederick Law Olmsted first defined Central Park and other first-generation public parks as artworks that must be appreciated through passive leisure activities such as pastoral strolls and quiet carriage rides. Moreover, he invented an elitist idea of appreciating nature and argued that one's level of cultural sophistication closely corresponded with the ability to recognize the value and beauty of nature. Olmsted's park philosophy was far more elitist and paternalist compared to those of John Claudius Loudon and Joseph Paxton, pioneering English park planners who aggressively advocated for working-class recreation and sports.[7] After the creation of Central Park, Olmsted dominated park planning in the U.S. for the next three decades and played a crucial role in solidifying his paternalistic and elitist beliefs within community and urban parks.[8]

White conservation elites also declared that wildlands, such as national parks, should provide space where White males could test their physical and mental strengths through the conquest of rugged natural environments and domination of wild animals, establishing a culture of masculine militarism in the parks.[9] Elites also legitimized sport hunting and fishing as the most ideal and sophisticated forms of outdoor activities. Concomitantly, they rejected the subsistence and market hunting and fishing that were popular among

Indigenous peoples, African Americans, Mexicans, and the working-class, portraying them as uncivilized and abusive of natural resources.[10] During the postwar era, furthermore, editors of major outdoor recreation magazines used militaristic and misogynistic rhetoric to problematize and discourage women's participation in hunting, so that they could capitalize on the large number of war veterans for the hunting industry.[11]

Through these arbitrary conceptualizations and legitimizations, White elites set the tone for what authentic and respectful park behaviors and outdoor recreation practices look like. Thus, from the very beginning, public parks in the United States were built as a space where the mores of White middle- and upper-class individuals were imposed on other demographic groups.[12] Although the White elites' conceptualization and legitimization of their own favored behaviors have been increasingly challenged by park researchers and practitioners, they remain prevalent in contemporary American society.[13]

2. Rules and Regulations

The arbitrary conceptualization and legitimization of White elites led to the creation of specific park and conservation rules that criminalized the park use and outdoor recreation of the working-class and people of color whose park activities tended to be more practical, utilitarian, and subsistence-oriented. Once Central Park was created, for example, Olmsted developed park regulations to prohibit any sport, vigorous recreation activity, or working-class leisure such as drinking, gambling, and large social gatherings. Indeed, Olmsted held a rigid paternalistic reformist ideology and was almost obsessed with educating the masses about civility and decorum. After resigning from the Central Park administration in 1861, Olmsted took a job as the manager of the Mariposa Estate, a gold-mining company near Yosemite in California. Olmsted cut the wages of miners to stabilize the budget, but it precipitated a violent strike. Olmsted not only had warrants issued for arresting protesting miners, but also proposed the construction of a reading and coffee room stocked with British and American periodicals. He believed that the coffee room would help miners stay away from alcohol and gambling and learn about civility. To him, public parks were ideal "classrooms" to educate the working-class and immigrants.[14]

Similarly, the establishment of state and national parks required new regulations for natural resource management. Inevitably, the new regulations criminalized and restricted the traditional subsistence activities of mountain and forest residents and Indigenous peoples that were intimately tied to their very survival. As Karl Jacoby astutely explained, those new parks and conservation regulations made "hunting or fishing redefined as poaching, foraging as trespassing, the setting of fires as arson, and the cutting of trees as timber theft."[15]

3. Policing and Surveillance

The creation of new park regulations meant that somebody had to enforce them. Contrary to the common belief that public parks offer peaceful respite and wholesome recreation, they have always been the site of in-depth policing and surveillance.[16] In conjunction with his park regulations, Olmsted developed a park police force and ordered them to gently enforce the rules to promote a contemplative atmosphere and prevent park users from taking trees, flowers, and stones in Central Park.[17] This was yet another example of park pioneers in the U.S. using parks as a moral and cultural fix for working-class people and people of color and a means to "Americanize" immigrants.[18]

In 1886, the Forest Commission in New York created forest police by hiring experienced woodsmen to patrol the newly created Forest Preserve in the Adirondack and Catskill Mountains. As the police enforced new conservation rules, longtime inhabitants were increasingly frustrated because their subsistence activities were criminalized, causing numerous skirmishes between the two groups. By contrast, wealthy tourists and seasonal vacationers who owned properties in the Adirondacks—which became a state park in 1892—favored enforcement because they believed it would ensure less disruption in the forest scenery and hunting games, providing tourism experiences that they wanted.[19]

U.S. Army soldiers were the first park rangers in national parks. After the establishment of Yellowstone National Park, the Department of the Interior was not able to protect the vast park effectively and, in 1886, called upon the Department of War for assistance.[20] Later, the same approach was used for managing Sequoia and Yosemite National Parks. Although soldiers provided critical aid to the environmental protection of newly created national parks, it is undeniable that they also contributed to the marginalization of Indigenous peoples and nearby White residents who depended on the parks' natural resources for their very survival.[21] Some researchers have pointed out that because of the historical criminalization of people of color by police, the presence of law enforcement in national parks does not help attracting diverse visitors.[22]

4. Location

Park and government officials have strategically selected park locations to disenfranchise the working-class and people of color. They built community and urban parks close to affluent White neighborhoods and far away from the poor and immigrants, making access to parks time-consuming and costly.[23] Similarly, during the first half of the 20th century in the Southern states, state park officials stymied African Americans' park use by building Negro Areas, or segregated park facilities, in places that were far away from major cities and poor in quality, both aesthetically and functionally.[24]

94 *Violent and Verdant*

Moreover, some racist policymakers and park leaders strategically used park construction as a tool to erase communities of color, displace the residents, and demarcate or reinforce residential racial segregation.[25] For example, Osh Kosh Camp was the oldest Indigenous neighborhood in Rapid City, South Dakota. When it was destroyed by a flood in 1972, city officials ignored Indigenous groups' housing needs and decided to create a park on the floodplain. Today, Founders Park near downtown Rapid City does not mention the history of Osh Kosh Camp and only celebrates early White settlers.[26]

Similarly, as illustrated in the opening quotes of the current chapter, the displacement of local residents through park construction, a phenomenon often labeled as green gentrification, is ongoing in American society. Green gentrification tends to induce significant displacement pressure through increased property taxes as well as changes in community atmosphere and dynamics that make existing residents feel out of place.[27]

5. Design

Parks' design features have also added to the disenfranchisement of marginalized groups. For the first generation of community parks, park planners used trees and bodies of water to create a clear spatial separation between parks and cities. Again, the intention here was to legitimize activities that emphasized privacy, solitude, and contemplation as the most respectful ways of using parks and appreciating their natural environment while rejecting the leisure activities of the poor and immigrants.[28]

State officials also used specific infrastructure to create clear racial boundaries in state parks. During the first half of the 20th century, the dual-use parks that were available to both Whites and Blacks ensured the greatest degree of racial separation through separate access roads and landscape features such as tracts of forest, lakes, and ponds that demarcated racial segregation.[29] Therefore, many parks' landscape design was more than aesthetic: It was imbued with specific, and sometimes malicious, intent.

6. Deceptive Narratives or "Greensplaining"

Affluent and influential government officials, businessmen, and leaders of environmental and conservation organizations often deploy a series of narratives to further their own agendas. These narratives emphasize the environmental, economic, and health benefits of new park projects while conveniently obscuring the parks' damaging effects, such as gentrification and displacement, on disadvantaged communities. For the elite, the goal is to attain broader public, political, and media support for the park project and smuggle in a variety of gentrifying and culturally suppressing actions against minoritized groups.[30] This narrative technique is what Fernandez and colleagues conceptualized as "greensplaining"—a rhetorical and deceptive communication strategy that helps justify new park projects and perpetuates class and race privilege.[31]

7. Discriminatory Laws and Customs

Historically, discriminatory laws were the most blatant exclusionary measure against people of color in American public parks. Under Jim Crow, individuals' access to parks depended on their racial and ethnic backgrounds, and noncompliance with those laws would result in legal punishment or White retaliation.[32] Even if discriminatory laws did not exist in some areas, deeply rooted racial prejudice among the majority of White Americans functioned as unwritten rules. People of color were routinely ordered or threatened by park officials and White park users either to leave or use segregated sections of the parks.[33] Notably, these discriminatory laws and customs were not limited to the Southern states or the Jim Crow Era, but were prevalent across the nation until the second half of the 20th century.[34]

8. Terrorism

For centuries, racist Americans have used verbal abuse, intimidation, harassment, physical attacks, lynching, and vandalism to prevent people of color's access to public parks. For instance, when Fairground Park in St. Louis, Missouri opened its outdoor swimming pool to both White and Black children in 1949, about 200 angry White children and men, armed with bats, clubs, bricks, and knives, gathered outside the pool and began shouting threats to Black swimmers. Seven police officers arrived at the pool to escort the Black children, yet provided no adequate protection. The situation escalated into the Fairground Park Riot where hundreds of police officers had to be dispatched and 12 individuals were hospitalized.[35] In 1946, after Buder Park in Missouri was transformed from a White playground to an African American playground, Ku Klux Klan members burned a ten-foot tall cross and left behind a white hood with the letters "KKK" emblazoned across the brow.[36] In 1948, the gates at Booker T. Washington State Park in Tennessee, one of two state parks available for Blacks and mainly built by Black units of the CCC, were chopped down twice, likely by White vandals.[37] This is just a small sample of the White terrorism committed against people of color in public parks.

9. Privatization

Privatization was one of the most popular strategies of White racists to keep public parks off-limits to the poor and people of color, especially during the 20th century. When the pressure to desegregate public parks was intensified during the Civil Rights Era, racist park and government officials frequently sold public parks to private entities to avoid the legal obligation to accommodate citizens of all racial and ethnic backgrounds. Sometimes those private entities were created by the officials or had close connections with them. Once the park was privatized, membership-based access was used to make it exclusive to Whites.[38]

10. Closure

Park closure was another common strategy of racist park and government officials. When they had few options to curtail people of color's access to public parks, they simply closed the parks, citing various reasons. For example, after the eruption of the Fairground Park Riot, St. Louis Mayor Joseph Darst closed the park. The park reopened in 1949, yet the city closed it again in 1956, once again taking recreational opportunities away from youth of color.[39] In South Carolina in 1963, the entire state park system was closed in order to boycott a court order to desegregate state parks. Clearly, many White Americans preferred complete closure of public parks to letting people of color enjoy them.[40]

11. Underfunding and Disinvestment

Parks and recreation programs offered in communities of the poor, people of color, and immigrants have historically been underfunded. Andrew Kahrl and Malcolm Cammeron noted that there was continuing disinvestment in urban communities from the New Deal project of the 1930s through the Nixon administration of the 1970s. For example, during the 1960s, newly established programs and organizations such as the Open Space Land Program, the Bureau of Outdoor Recreation, and the Land and Water Conservation Fund Act all focused on developing parks and recreation infrastructure for rural and suburban residents who were predominantly middle-class White Americans. From 1962 to 1974, the Open Space Land Program helped American cities obtain 348,000 acres of urban open space through $442 million of grants, yet merely 6% of them ($17.7 million) were allocated toward the park building and restoration in low-income urban communities.[41] This type of historical disinvestment in communities of color is often coupled with discriminatory federal policies such as redlining, resulting in the concentration of large parks and high quality greenspaces in White middle- and upper-class neighborhoods.[42]

12. Naming and Monument Building

There is no easier way to exert symbolic and cultural exclusionary pressure on people of color than to simply name a park after notorious racists, eugenicists, KKK members, or Confederate generals. In Helena, Montana in 1916, for example, the United Daughters of the Confederacy, a neo-Confederacy organization consisting of female descendants of Confederate

Civil War soldiers, donated a water fountain to the city's Great Northern Park (now called Hill Park). Engraved on the fountain was the text, "A loving tribute to our Confederate Soldiers," making it the northernmost Confederate memorial in the U.S. until 1926. James Loewen criticized that Montana never had any Confederate or Union soldiers, because most of Montana was still Indian country and not even a territory during most of the Civil War. He further stressed that the Daughters deliberately placed monuments and statues across the nation from the 1890s to the 1940s to signify continuing Confederate power and to imply that the Confederacy was somehow patriotic.[43]

13. Erasure or Omission of Legacies

While the legacy of notorious racists was actively promoted through naming and monument building, the legacy of marginalized people was frequently erased and omitted in public parks. For instance, Cedar Hill State Park in Texas was portrayed as a pastoral farmland of an agricultural family and none of the park's interpretive or marketing materials mentioned that several family members who donated the parkland were slaveowners.[44] In the Adirondack Park in New York, even though incarcerated workers from nearby correctional facilities made a critical contribution to the development and preservation of the park, this history is almost invisible in the region today.[45] Similarly, in the wilderness designated area of Congaree National Park in South Carolina, there was no mention of the Black slaves who built Buyck's Cattle Ring, the only ring-shaped cattle mount known to exist in the United States. Also unmentioned was the historical presence of maroon settlements within the park, communities of people who escaped from slavery. In 2013, the park provided an educational program about the maroon community during its local heritage tourism event.[46] At Independence National Historical Park in Philadelphia, there were no historical interpretations of "the people who built the buildings (African Americans), who financed the Revolution (Jewish Americans), or who fed the soldiers (women, mothers, and wives)."[47]

14. Commercialization

The notion that American public parks, especially national parks, were created to rescue the degenerating natural environment from private development is a hoax. The truth is that commercialism and commodification deeply intersected with the parks' origin story. The commercial interests of railroad and tourism companies propelled the development of national parks such as Yosemite and Yellowstone, and the Department of the Interior also supported commercial activities within national parks to attract more tourists.[48] Until national parks became more accessible through the popularization of automobiles, national parks were mainly enjoyed by people who could afford long and expensive vacations.

98   *Violent and Verdant*

Recently, critics argued that the influx of private funding in new park developments has tainted the identity of parks as public and democratic spaces. They have documented that the encroachment of commercialism and capitalism onto the parks, such as incorporating fancy retail stores and artisanal restaurants and cafés, gave rise to the implicit yet distinct exclusionary pressure on people who are unwilling or unable to consume.[49] In his investigation of postindustrial park projects in three major cities in the U.S., Kevin Loughran (2022) concluded that,

> It is about consuming landscapes and products and food and experiences. Being the kind of person who has not only the leisure time to visit a park but the good taste and right disposition to admire picturesque postindustrial views and consume artisanal food and drink. Others can visit the parks, of course, but the layers of privilege and exclusion make it very clear who these spaces are meant for.[50]

The Ongoing Fight Against Park Injustice: 13 Counterstrategies

Systemic park injustice has been tyrannical, yet many people have fought back and continue to do so today. As we witnessed from the previous chapters, Indigenous peoples, Black Americans, immigrants, and the working-class bravely resisted violence and oppression from the White ruling class. This history of struggle and resistance is hardly over. In contemporary America, park researchers, practitioners, and activists have developed several counterstrategies against long-lasting and pervasive park injustices to protect vulnerable and marginalized groups. These measures differ in scope and context, ranging from specific micro-level solutions to recommendations for high-level tactics. Below, I summarize 13 counterstrategies that have resisted park injustice.

1. Affordable Housing Programs

New park developments that have the admirable goal of providing greenspace to communities of the poor and people of color can in fact cause gentrification, thus displacing longtime residents via increased rent and property taxes as well as changes to the community atmosphere. As such, park researchers and practitioners have argued that providing affordable housing is crucial to prevent displacement and ensure that existing residents would benefit from new parks.[51] Establishing nonprofit or government agencies (often called Community Land Trusts) to address affordable housing and fair community development is also effective in preventing green gentrification and in stabilizing housing affordability.[52]

To make affordable housing programs work, the programs must provide sufficient housing units in relation to park size—a provision they must initiate at the early stage of park planning, before the property values increase. Additionally, the creation of affordable housing units can be coupled with inclusionary zoning policies which stipulate that the developers allocate a certain portion of the land for affordable housing.[53]

2. Grants and Financial Support Programs

To date, various grants and financial support programs have been developed to make public parks more widely accessible. The Outdoor Recreation Legacy Partnership (ORLP), a nationwide, dollar-for-dollar matching grant program, was established in 2014 to help historically underserved urban communities that lack access to public parks and outdoor recreation spaces. Since then, the ORLP program has distributed funds through the National Park Service (NPS) and has supported many new park projects in multiple states. In December 2023, for example, the Department of the Interior announced that NPS would distribute $21.9 million for the redevelopment or creation of new local parks in five states. Significantly, the announcement added that the ORLP program would provide more than $224 million the following year, the largest grant funding since the launch of the program.[54]

Although this large investment in public parks from the federal government is desirable, new park projects in historically park-deprived communities can trigger gentrification and inflict greater financial stress to nearby renters, homeowners, and small businesses via increased property values and taxes. In response, a multitude of financial support programs have been developed, such as rent control and anti-eviction protection, property tax freezes, and tax credits and low-interest loan programs for small businesses.[55] Some programs focus on providing financial or tax incentives to park developers, so that they can develop sufficient affordable housing units near parks.[56] Other programs, such as hiring ordinances, focus more on providing economic opportunities to residents, prioritizing their hiring in the construction and maintenance of new parks.[57]

Moreover, many municipal park and recreation agencies and environmental organizations have provided financial support to historically disenfranchised communities, encouraging residents' visitation to existing parks. Those financial supports include free park passes, free camping experiences, and invitations to outdoor recreation or education programs held in parks. Some of these programs are geared toward youth and children of historically disenfranchised communities. The idea is to rectify the historical park injustice by cultivating park stewardship and outdoor recreation knowledge among younger generations. Youth programs have been advocated as a promising long-term strategy to break the historically reproductive pattern of park injustice.[58]

3. Community Benefits Agreements (CBAs)

Community Benefits Agreements (CBAs) are legal contracts between private park developers and community members (or their coalitions), typically with the involvement or assistance of local government actors, in major development projects. As such, CBAs can entail a variety of economic, environmental, and social issues related to park development. These may include establishing affordable housing, creating a community fund, prioritizing local hires, developing community facilities, and remediating traffic, noise, and pollution.[59]

CBAs emerged during the late 1990s as a mechanism for vulnerable local communities to work directly with other parties and ultimately influence the process and outcome of new developments. The flexibility of CBAs allows community members to negotiate various issues associated with park projects and help them gain full benefits from new park developments. However, CBAs can also lead to delays or increased project costs when legal validity and enforceability are unclear and complicated.[60] Another caveat is that private developers can take advantage of CBAs to purchase public support with benefits that are insufficient or inadequate to compensate local communities.[61] Still, when done thoughtfully, CBAs can be valuable to all stakeholders in park developments and empower minoritized communities.

4. Community Benefits Funds (CBFs)

Recognizing some limitations in the structure and implementation of previous CBAs in large-scale developments in American cities, Bridget Vance proposed Community Benefits Funds (CBFs) as an alternative funding mechanism for the benefit of community members who are directly affected by new developments. CBFs are slightly different from the traditional Grants and Financial Support Programs (#2), in that community members have more control over the funds. The city first creates a fund in the form of a nonprofit corporation, which will be sourced through real property taxes from the project or a required payment by the project to the community fund in lieu of taxes for a fixed period. The corporation would create a board of directors comprised of representatives from the city, who would be charged with determining the use of the fund. Additionally, clear guidelines and policies regarding the provision of the fund as well as annual reports and quarterly meetings open to the public would be required. Vance (2018) argued that CBFs are "a community equity strategy that incorporates principles of accountability, transparency, fairness, feasibility, monitoring, and enforceability."[62]

5. Community Participation

Park researchers and practitioners have commonly endorsed community participation as one of the most important and just approaches in the development and management of public parks and urban greenspaces. The community participation approach significantly varies by method (e.g., survey, interview, town-hall meeting, vote, serving on a board or committee) and level of involvement (superficial and short-term vs. in-depth and long-term).[63] Despite the variation, the gist of this approach is to include existing residents or stakeholders in the decision-making process and empower them as co-creators, co-designers, and co-managers of public parks.[64] To this end, the community participation approach often goes along with educational programs and workshops to increase different stakeholders' awareness of park planning and management and to strengthen their social, economic, and political capacity.[65]

Community participation also has some shortcomings, however. First, since marginalized communities often lack time, resources, and expertise in park development or management, demanding their participation could be more burdensome than empowering. Second, even though community participation is meant to be an alternative to the top-down approach in park development, it could reinforce the vulnerable position of some groups if more powerful developers and the state do not distribute sufficient decision-making power.[66] Despite these limitations, the community participation approach is advocated as an effective strategy for avoiding park injustice and producing several positive outcomes such as promoting shared governance, preventing gentrification and displacement, and empowering local communities.

6. Building Coalitions and Partnerships

Historically minoritized communities tend to lack resources and expertise to influence new park developments or effectively cope with systemic park injustice induced by powerful elite groups, corporate private developers, and government entities. As such, it is important for communities to strategically build coalitions with civil rights activists, advocacy groups, and environmental organizations to fight against park injustice and prevent further marginalization.[67] Moreover, building a multi-stakeholder partnership between private developers, public officials, NGOs, and community members allows all parties to address common problems collaboratively, share their resources and know-how, and promote shared governance.[68] Similar to the Community Participation approach (#5), there have been a multitude of different ways to design and structure coalition and partnership building.[69]

7. Creating Informal and Smaller Parks

Informal Green Space (IGS) denotes small green spaces in the city such as abandoned industrial sites, vacant lots, street or railway verges, brownfields, and linear residual green spaces alongside traffic infrastructure and waterways. Although IGS is different from public parks, since it is not recognized or managed by public entities, studies have documented that IGS is less prone to green gentrification, more easily accessible than large-scale parks, and still conducive to ecological, environmental, cultural, and recreational benefits offered by public parks. Accordingly, IGS has emerged as a more equitable and effective greening strategy in urban spaces where securing large parkland is challenging.[70] Some researchers noted that one IGS strategy that is particularly beneficial and empowering to existing residents is community gardens owned and managed by the city and/or community members.[71]

8. Developing a More Diverse and Inclusive Workforce

The parks and recreation workforce in the U.S. has been dominated by White individuals. In 2020, Whites accounted for 79% of full-time permanent employees of the NPS, which is down only 4% in 45 years.[72] Moreover, the U.S. Bureau of Labor Statistics reported that 78% of park and recreation employees were White.[73] Similarly, a recent study on park agency directors and policymakers in Pennsylvania showed that 97% of the study sample were White.[74] Alarmed by lingering White dominance in the industry, many park and recreation agencies have implemented various hiring programs to diversify their workforce.[75]

While White dominance in the field of parks and recreation is not at all surprising given the centuries of park injustice, the issue is also linked to White dominance in park and recreation programs in colleges and universities, that educate its future workforce. Mowatt and colleagues found that faculty, undergraduates, and graduates in parks, recreation, and tourism programs in U.S. universities were "embarrassingly White" and underscored a serious need for recruiting, retaining, and promoting people of color in academic leisure studies programs.[76] Similarly, Terry Sharik and colleagues noted that African Americans represented 3.2% and 2.7% of all undergraduate enrollment for forestry and natural resource programs, respectively.[77] While diversifying the racial and ethnic profile of the park and recreation industry and university programs is critical for moving away from the historical White dominance, it is also important that employees of color be hired and trained for managerial positions in order to foster equitable resource allocation and decision-making.[78]

9. Highlighting the History of Marginalized Communities

Highlighting the history of marginalized communities and their contributions to public parks can help disrupt the White hegemony in parks and outdoor recreation. Even though public parks were mainly built by White elites, it is important to note that the working-class, women, people of color, and immigrants were not simply victims of historical park injustice, but active users and creators of parks who have demonstrated remarkable agency in promoting democratic access and cultural diversity within public parks.

For example, although sport and vigorous physical activities were prohibited in Central Park, working-class and immigrant New Yorkers repeatedly questioned the legitimacy of such rules and, eventually, succeeded in creating baseball fields and spaces for other games and sports.[79] Industry workers, immigrants, and African Americans also provided critical financial, political, and labor support for the development of Indiana Dunes State Park in Indiana and wilderness parks outside Chicago and actively used the parks for recreation, religious, and political activities.[80] In Chicago, despite prevailing racial discrimination, African Americans fought for equal access in public parks and continued to use them not only to reconnect with their Southern identity, but also to escape from urban problems and experience nature as a place for leisure rather than labor.[81]

Enslaved African Americans' contribution to the development of Mammoth Cave National Park in Kentucky is also noteworthy. Stephen Bishop drafted one of the most comprehensive cave maps and Masterson "Mat" Bransford and Nick Bransford served as the first cave guides.[82] During the early 1920s, Matt Bransford, the grandson of Mat Bransford, and his wife, Zemmie Bransford, turned their home into the Bransford Summer Resort to accommodate Black visitors who could not stay at the Mammoth Cave Hotel and offered cave tours, that were kept secret from White patrons.[83]

Moreover, Buffalo Soldiers, African American cavalry units in the U.S. Army, commanded by Captain Charles Young, the third African American to graduate from the U.S. Military Academy and the first Black national park superintendent, were the first park rangers who served in Yosemite, Sequoia, and General Grant (now Kings Canyon) National Parks during the late 19th and early 20th centuries.[84] Many civil rights activists also fought against Black exclusion in public parks. For example, William J. Trent Jr., an African American civil rights activist who served as an adviser of Negro Affairs for Interior Secretary Harold L. Ickes, fought for increased African American access to parks, which led to the ending of racial segregation in national parks in 1942.[85]

The pioneering work, courageous resistance, and remarkable agency of marginalized communities is nothing short of extraordinary. These stories are not only culturally and historically important, but also teem with ingenuity, courage, and the kind of pioneering spirit that all Americans should admire. These stories need to be more widely celebrated in park interpretive, programming, marketing, and educational materials if we hope to end historical park injustice.

10. *Renaming of Parks or Removal of Statues*

Since the Civil Rights era in the 1960s, there has been an ongoing effort to change the names of places, buildings, or organizations named after slaveowners, racists, or Confederate generals. This effort gained significant momentum in the early 21st century following White supremacist Dylann Roof's mass shooting at an African American church in Charleston, South Carolina in 2015, as well as the murder of George Floyd, an African American man, by police in Minneapolis in 2020. A report released by the Southern

Poverty Law Center noted that 168 Confederate symbols were renamed or removed from public spaces in 2020 alone.[86]

Public parks have been a significant battleground in this renaming and removal movement. Recently, some NPS units have decided to change place names to highlight Indigenous heritage or acknowledge histories of racial exclusion and White supremacy.[87] In 2017, the Confederate water fountain in Helena, mentioned in the Naming and Monument Building (#12) section of this chapter, was removed from the city. Alarmed by Roof's mass shooting in 2015, city commissioners Katharine Haque-Hausrath and Andres Halladay proposed "rededicating" the fountain, arguing that the city does not need a Confederate memorial that symbolizes support for slavery and White supremacy.[88]

Similarly, in 2017 the Memorial to the Confederate Dead in Forest Park in St. Louis, was permanently removed from the city's largest public park, and its ownership was transferred to the Missouri Civil War Museum. The agreement between the city, the museum, and the United Daughters of the Confederacy stipulates that the monument will not be publicly displayed in the city or St. Louis County at any time in the future and its placement will be limited to a Civil War museum, battlefield, or cemetery.[89]

Robert E. Lee Park in Dallas, Texas is another example. It was originally built as a private park named Oak Lawn Park in 1903, and the city purchased it in 1909. In 1928, the Dallas Southern Memorial Association began plans for placing Lee's statue in the park. Eight years later, the statue was unveiled by President Franklin D. Roosevelt, and the park was renamed after the Confederate general. In 2017, the statue was removed, and two years later, the park was renamed Turtle Creek Park.[90]

In 2020, the Christopher Columbus monument in Fred G. Bond Metro Park in the town of Cary, North Carolina, was vandalized and then removed. It was a gift from the Knights of Columbus to the town in 1992, celebrating the 500th anniversary of Columbus's "landing" in the Americas, yet the word "landing" was marked off and replaced with "invasion." The Knights requested the monument to be returned, and the town decided to do so.[91]

11. Challenging Existing Park Culture

As you learned in previous chapters, White middle-and upper-class mores, rooted in colonialism and environmentalism, have shaped public parks, conversation ideologies and practices, and outdoor recreation in the U.S. Those in power legitimized solitary, exploratory, and passive appreciation of parks—which excluded the experiences of many Indigenous, working-class, and African American visitors. Although such culture has faded somewhat over time, it has by no means disappeared. In fact, empirical studies have repeatedly documented that outdoor recreation activities of White Americans tend to focus on solitude seeking, independence, and expedition, while those of people of color are more collectivistic and center on relationship and community building.[92]

Recently, there has been a heightened awareness within Black communities about the White colonial legacy in outdoor recreation and a growing effort to recognize and nurture African Americans' authentic experience with parks and nature.[93] Demographic changes taking place in the U.S. indicate that by the mid-2040s, the nation will become a so-called "majority-minority society" where White Americans will become a numerical minority.[94] In this context, the legitimacy of "proper" park use established by White elites will be more frequently contested. For park and recreation agencies, balancing different recreational orientations among diverse population groups is becoming an increasingly challenging, yet critical task.

12. Affinity Groups

People of color have established outdoor recreation affinity groups so they can feel more comfortable and safe and help more people of color enjoy outdoor recreation. Some of them include Outdoor Afro, Latino Outdoors, and Melanin Base Camp. Although these groups were established in the 2000s and 2010s, others have a much longer history. For example, Slippers-N-Sliders Ski Club was established in Colorado in 1972 as a non-profit organization and is still in operation.[95]

13. The Land Back Movement

The Land Back Movement (LBM) denotes a social and political movement advocating for the return of stolen or appropriated Indigenous ancestral homelands to promote Indigenous sovereignty and self-determination.[96] Although the land return would hardly undo the historical colonization, genocide, displacement, and enslavement of Indigenous peoples, there have been several successful cases of land return, dating back to the 1970s. Thus, even though transferring the ownership of a large tract of land, such as a national park, may sound unrealistic or too complicated to be actualized, legal researchers have pointed out that it is not impossible, and even in some cases, Indigenous communities gradually bought back their lands.[97] Moreover, even if land return is practically unfeasible, making colonizers pay rent or contribute to land trusts has been viewed as an alternative reparation.[98] Kevin Washburn, former Assistant Secretary of Indian Affairs, noted that "a simple path to tribal co-management [of public lands] already exists in federal law. It has been authorized by Congress for more than twenty-five years and required no significant new congressional action."[99]

The co-management of public lands with Indigenous peoples has been a distinctive segment of the broad LBM.[100] There have been several successful co-management agreements between NPS units and Indigenous communities, and the agreements generally aim to promote the return or improvement of the land governance authority of Indigenous peoples by adopting their traditional ecological knowledge and land management practices.[101] The co-management approach is also desirable from a sustainability standpoint, because examples of Indigenous land stewardship from different countries have commonly shown that Indigenous environmental management is more sustainable and effective in coping with deforestation, habitat destruction, greenhouse gas emissions, and climate change.[102] The effectiveness of Indigenous land management over European and American management is not surprising, given that Indigenous peoples tamed and cultivated nature for millennia before European colonization.

Resistance, Struggles, and Agitation

The whole history of the progress of human liberty shows that all concessions yet made to her august claims have been born of earnest struggle...If there is no struggle, there is no progress. Those who profess to favor freedom and yet deprecate agitation are men who want crops without plowing the ground... Power concedes nothing without a demand. It never has and it never will...The limits of tyrants are prescribed by the endurance of those whom they oppress.
Frederick Douglass, his address on West India Emancipation on August 4, 1857[103]

Systemic park injustice is deep-seated and monstrous, yet the people have fought back with unyielding determination. In his famous address in 1857, Frederick Douglass underscored that the progress of human liberty is not handed out for free, but must be won through relentless struggles and agitations against oppressive tyrants. His words on liberty are especially powerful and inspirational, considering Douglass's own journey: He was born as an enslaved man, but was determined to educate himself, risking his life multiple times, and eventually escaped from bondage in 1838 when he was in his early 20s.[104] Without his courage and perseverance for justice and liberty, he could not have become a freeman and rise as one of the most prominent abolitionists and Civil Rights activists in American history.

Douglass' message profoundly resonates with the history of public parks in the U.S. Parks represent the tyranny of the ruling class, yet they also symbolize ordinary people's unceasing fight for justice and liberty. From Indigenous peoples fighting against colonists in Yosemite or Yellowstone regions and working-class immigrants demanding baseball fields in Central Park, to African Americans resisting racial segregation in public parks and the mountain communities in Appalachia battling for fair compensation for displacement, the history of American public parks is a chronicle of the people's struggle, courage, and pursuit of full humanity. Many times, the people lost their battles, crushed by the powerful logic of park injustice. But there were also victories, creating pathbreaking changes in public parks such as more equal and democratic access, removal of Confederate statues, and massive government investments for more parks and greenspaces in historically underserved communities. This is precisely why we must keep fighting.

As we wage this historic battle against systemic park injustice, I argue that we must go beyond our immediate struggles in public parks and more critically interrogate the broader social context in which this injustice took root and thrived. That is, while the White ruling class were the ones who developed and implemented systemic park injustice, they were able to do so more effectively and efficiently within certain cultural, economic, and political systems, namely capitalism, colonialism, elitism, racism, and sexism. In other words, the key to ending this prolonged battle may lie hidden behind those backdrops. In the next chapter, I extend our battle to the backdrops.

Notes

1 Brandon Harris et al., "Contested spaces: Intimate segregation and environmental gentrification on Chicago's 606 trail," *City & Community* 19, no. 4 (2020): 948.
2 Housing Justice League and Research|Action Cooperative, *BeltLining: Gentrification, broken promises, and hope on Atlanta's southside* (2017), 35, Retrieved from https://static1.squarespace.com/static/59da49b712abd904963589b6/t/59dedb75f7e0ab47a08224b5/1507777424592/Beltlining+Report+-+HJL+and+RA+Oct+9.pdf.
3 Nufar Avni, "Bridging equity? Washington, DC's new elevated park as a test case for just planning," *Urban Geography* 40, no. 4 (2019): 10.
4 Brandon Harris, Alessandro Rigolon, and Mariela Fernandez, "'To them, we're just kids from the hood': Citizen-based policing of youth of color, 'white space,' and environmental gentrification," *Cities* 107 (2020); Harris et al., "Contested spaces"; Geoff Smith et al., *Measuring the impact of the 606: Understanding how a large public investment impacted the surrounding housing market*, Institute for Housing Studies at DePaul University (2016), https://www.housingstudies.org/media/filer_public/2016/10/31/ihs_measuring_the_impact_of_the_606.pdf.
5 Dan Immergluck, "Atlanta's BeltLine shows how urban parks can drive 'green gentrification' if cities don't think about affordable housing at the start," *The Conversation* (2023). https://theconversation.com/atlantas-beltline-shows-how-urban-parks-can-drive-green-gentrification-if-cities-dont-think-about-affordable-housing-at-the-start-193204; Dan Immergluck and Tharunya Balan, "Sustainable for whom? Green urban development, environmental gentrification, and the Atlanta Beltline," *Urban geography* 39, no. 4 (2018); Jessica Martínez, "'ARE WE JUST KILLING PEOPLE?': Centering Racial Capitalism in the Green Gentrification of the Atlanta BeltLine," *International Journal of Urban and Regional Research* 47, no. 3 (2023). For the income inequality, see Andrew DePietro, "20 Cities With The Worst Income Inequality In America In 2022," *Forbes*, 2022, https://www.forbes.com/sites/andrewdepietro/2022/03/31/20-cities-with-the-worst-income-inequality-in-america-in-2022/?sh=2d6c17ae608b.
6 Avni, "Bridging equity?"
7 Denby, Jonathan. "Gardeners and the Democratisation of Urban Parks." *Landscape History* 45, no. 1 (2024).
8 Dorceta E. Taylor, "Central Park as a model for social control: urban parks, social class and leisure behavior in nineteenth-century America," *Journal of Leisure Research* 31, no. 4 (1999); Wendy Harding, "Frederick Law Olmsted's Failed Encounter with Yosemite and the Invention of a Proto-Environmentalist," *Ecozon* 5, no. 1 (2014); Roy Rosenzweig and Elizabeth Blackmar, *The Park and the People: A History of Central Park* (Cornell University Press, 1998), Chapter 5.
9 Dorceta E. Taylor, *The Rise of the American Conservation Movement: Power, Privilege, and Environmental Protection* (Duke University Press, 2016), Chapter 3, 346.
10 Scott E. Giltner, *Hunting and Fishing in the New South: Black Labor and White Leisure after the Civil War* (Johns Hopkins University Press, 2008), Chapter 2; Karl Jacoby, *Crimes against nature: Squatters, Poachers, Thieves, and the Hidden History of American Conservation* (University of California Press, 2014).
11 KangJae Jerry Lee, Rudy Dunlap, and Michael B. Edwards, "The implication of Bourdieu's Theory of Practice for leisure studies," *Leisure Sciences* 36, no. 3 (2014); A.L. Smalley, "'I just like to kill things': women, men and the gender

of sport hunting in the United States, 1940–1973," *Gender & History* 17, no. 1 (2005).
12 Jason Byrne and Jennifer Wolch, "Nature, race, and parks: past research and future directions for geographic research," *Progress in Human Geography* 33, no. 6 (2009); Denis Cosgrove, "Habitable earth: Wilderness, empire, and race in America," in *Wild Ideas*, ed. D. Rothenberg (University of Minnesota Press, 1995); KangJae Jerry Lee et al., "Slow violence in public parks in the U.S.: can we escape our troubling past?" *Social & Cultural Geography* 24, no. 7 (2023).
13 Harrison P. Pinckney et al., "'We have our own cultural ways of being in nature': New perspectives on African Americans' relationships to U.S. National Parks," *Journal of Leisure Research* (2024); Carolyn Finney, *Black Faces, White Spaces: Reimagining the Relationship of African Americans to the Great Outdoors* (UNC Press, 2014).
14 Rosenzweig and Blackmar, *The Park and the People*, Chapter 9; David Thacher, "Olmsted's Police," *Law and History Review* 33, no. 3 (2015). For Olmsted's work in the Mariposa Estate, see Stephen Germic, *American Green: Class, Crisis, and the Deployment of Nature in Central Park, Yosemite, and Yellowstone* (Lexington Books, 2001), 53–55.
15 Jacoby, *Crimes against Nature*, 2; Mark David Spence, *Dispossessing the Wilderness: Indian Removal and the Making of the National Parks* (Oxford University Press, 1999), 31.
16 Rasul A. Mowatt, "A People's Future of Leisure Studies: Fear City, Cop City and Others Tales, a Call for Police Research," *Leisure Sciences* 45, no. 5 (2023); Michael R. Pendleton, "Policing the Park: Understanding Soft Enforcement," *Journal of Leisure Research* 30, no. 4 (1998).
17 Thacher, "Olmsted's Police"; Rosenzweig and Blackmar, *The Park and the People*, 91.
18 Nate Gabriel, "The work that parks do: towards an urban environmentality," *Social & Cultural Geography* 12, no. 02 (2011); Kevin Loughran, "Urban parks and urban problems: An historical perspective on green space development as a cultural fix," *Urban Studies* 57, no. 11 (2020).
19 Jacoby, *Crimes against Nature*, Chpater 2.
20 Charles R. Farabee, *National Park Ranger: An American Icon* (Rowman & Littlefield, 2003), 9.
21 Jacoby, *Crimes against Nature*, Chapter 6; Spence, *Dispossessing the Wilderness*.
22 Akiebia S. Hicks et al., "When green is blue: Perspectives on inclusivity and recommendations towards reforming and demilitarizing law enforcement in US national parks," *Parks Stewardship Forum* 36, no. 3 (2020).
23 Rosenzweig and Blackmar, *The Park and the People*, 229; Galen Cranz, *The Politics of Park Design: A History of Urban Parks in America* (MIT Press, 1982), 30; Galen Cranz and Michael Boland, "Defininig the sustainable park: A fifth model for urban parks," *Landscape Journal* 23, no. 2 (2004): 103; Brian McCammack, *Landscapes of Hope: Nature and the Great Migration in Chicago* (Harvard University Press, 2017), 51–52.
24 William E. O'Brien, *Landscapes of Exclusion: State Parks and Jim Crow in the American South* (University of Massachusetts Press, 2016), 23, 49.
25 Kevin Loughran, "Race and the construction of city and nature," *Environment and Planning A* 49, no. 9 (2017); Antero Pietila, *Not in my Neighborhood: How Bigotry Shaped a Great American City* (Rowman & Littlefield, 2010), 51.

26 Stephen R. Hausmann, "Erasing Indian Country: Urban Native Space and the 1972 Rapid City Flood," *Western Historical Quarterly* 52, no. 3 (2021).
27 Kenneth Gould and Tammy Lewis, *Green Gentrification: Urban Sustainability and the Struggle for Environmental Justice* (Routledge, 2016); Hamil Pearsall, "New directions in urban environmental/green gentrification research," in *Handbook of Gentrification Studies*, eds. Loretta Lees and Martin Phillips (Edward Elgar Publishing, 2018); Alessandro Rigolon and Timothy Collins, "The green gentrification cycle," *Urban Studies* 60, no. 4 (2023).
28 Cranz, *The politics of park design*, Chapter 1; Loughran, "Urban parks and urban problems."
29 O'Brien, *Landscapes of exclusion*, 9.
30 Lauren E. Mullenbach, "Critical discourse analysis of urban park and public space development," *Cities* 120 (2022); Lauren E. Mullenbach, Andrew J. Mowen, and Kathryn J. Brasier, "Urban parks, the growth machine, and the media: An analysis of press coverage of the high line, klyde warren park, and the rail park," *Environmental Sociology* (2021); Alessandro Rigolon et al., "'A park is not just a park': Toward counter-narratives to advance equitable green space policy in the United States," *Cities* 128 (2022).
31 Mariela Fernandez, Brandon Harris, and Jeff Rose, "Greensplaining environmental justice: A narrative of race, ethnicity, and justice in urban greenspace development," *Journal of Race, Ethnicity and the City* 2, no. 2 (2021).
32 Myron F. Floyd and Rasul A. Mowatt, "Leisure among African Americans " in *Race, Ethnicity, and Leisure*, eds. Monika Stodolska et al. (Human Kinetics 2013).
33 McCammack, *Landscapes of Hope*, 30; O'Brien, *Landscapes of Exclusion*, 28; Victoria W. Wolcott, *Race, Riots, and Roller Coasters: The Struggle over Segregated Recreation in America* (University of Pennsylvania Press, 2012), 47.
34 Joe R. Feagin and Kimberley Ducey, *Racist America: Roots, Current Realities, and Future Reparations* (Routledge, 2018); Komozi Woodard and Jeanne Theoharis, *The Strange Careers of the Jim Crow North: Segregation and Struggle Outside of the South* (NYU Press, 2019).
35 Jeff Wiltse, *Contested Waters: A Social History of Swimming Pools in America* (University of North Carolina Press, 2007), 171–74.
36 Joseph Heathcott, "Black archipelago: Politics and civic life in the Jim Crow city," *Journal of Social History* 38, no. 3 (2005): 726.
37 O'Brien, *Landscapes of Exclusion*, 112.
38 O'Brien, *Landscapes of Exclusion*, Chapter 5: Wolcott, *Race, Riots, and Roller Coasters*, 76–77.
39 Wiltse, *Contested Waters*, 174; Walter Johnson, *The Broken Heart of America: St. Louis and the Violent History of the United States* (Basic Books, 2020), 264.
40 O'Brien, *Landscapes of Exclusion*, 142.
41 Andrew W. Kahrl and Malcolm Cammeron, *African American Outdoor Recreation* (U.S. Department of the Interior National Park Service, 2022), 111–12.
42 For the redlining, see Dexter H. Locke et al., "Residential housing segregation and urban tree canopy in 37 US Cities," *npj Urban Sustainability* 1, no. 1 (2021). For the policy decision and inequitable funding allocation, see Christopher G. Boone et al., "Parks and people: An environmental justice inquiry in Baltimore, Maryland," *Annals of the Association of American Geographers* 99, no. 4 (2009); Alessandro Rigolon and Jeremy Németh, "What Shapes Uneven Access to Urban Amenities? Thick Injustice and the Legacy of Racial Discrimination in Denver's Parks," *Journal of Planning Education and Research* 41, no. 3 (2018).

43 "1916 Confederate Soldiers' Memorial Fountain," n.d., accessed 9th April, 2024, http://www.helenahistory.org/confederate-fountain-hill-park.htm; James W. Loewen, *Lies across America: What Our Historic Sites Get Wrong* (The New Press, 2019), Chapter 15.
44 KangJae Jerry Lee and David Scott, "Bourdieu and African Americans' Park Visitation: The Case of Cedar Hill State Park in Texas," *Leisure Sciences* 38, no. 5 (2016).
45 Clarence Jefferson Hall, *A Prison in the Woods: Environment and Incarceration in New York's North Country* (University of Massachusetts Press, 2020).
46 Matthew A. Lockhart, "'The Trouble with Wilderness' Education in the National Park Service: The Case of the Lost Cattle Mounts of Congaree," *The Public Historian* 28, no. 2 (2006); Janae Davis, "Black faces, black spaces: Rethinking African American underrepresentation in wildland spaces and outdoor recreation," *Environment and Planning E: Nature and Space* 2, no. 1 (2019); "Celebrate SwampFest at Congaree," 2014, Retrieved on March 3, 2024 from www.nps.gov/cong/parknews/swampfest-2013.htm.
47 Setha M. Low et al., "Recapturing erased histories: Ethnicity, design, and cultural representation—A case study of Independence National Historical Park," *Journal of Architectural and Planning Research* 19, no. 4 (2002): 283.
48 Mark Daniel Barringer, *Selling Yellowstone: Capitalism and the Construction of Nature* (University Press of Kansas, 2002).
49 Andrew Smith, "Sustaining municipal parks in an era of neoliberal austerity: The contested commercialisation of Gunnersbury Park," *Environment and Planning A: Economy and Space* 53, no. 4 (2021).
50 Kevin Loughran, *Parks for Profit: Selling Nature in the City* (Columbia University Press, 2022), 167.
51 Gould and Lewis, *Green Gentrification*; Pearsall, "New directions"; Hamil Pearsall and Jillian K. Eller, "Locating the green space paradox: A study of gentrification and public green space accessibility in Philadelphia, Pennsylvania," *Landscape and Urban Planning* 195 (2020). For affordable housing, see Diane K. Levy, Jennifer Comey, and Sandra Padilla, "In the face of gentrification: Case studies of local efforts to mitigate displacement," *Journal of Affordable Housing & Community Development Law* (2007); Hamil Pearsall and Isabelle Anguelovski, "Contesting and resisting environmental gentrification: Responses to new paradoxes and challenges for urban environmental justice," *Sociological Research Online* 21, no. 3 (2016); Alessandro Rigolon and Jon Christensen, *Greening without Gentrification: Learning from Parks-Related Anti-displacement Strategies Nationwide*, (2019).
52 Myungshik Choi, Shannon Van Zandt, and David Matarrita-Cascante, "Can community land trusts slow gentrification?," *Journal of Urban Affairs* 40, no. 3 (2018).
53 For the early initiation, see Alessandro Rigolon et al., "More than 'just green enough': helping park professionals achieve equitable greening and limit environmental gentrification," *Journal of Park & Recreation Administration* 38, no. 3 (2020). For the zoning, see Levy, Comey, and Padilla, "In the face of gentrification."; Rigolon and Christensen, *Greening without gentrification: learning from parks-related anti-displacement strategies nationwide*.
54 "Outdoor Recreation Legacy Partnership Grants Program," n.d., Retrieved on May 2, 2024 from https://www.nps.gov/subjects/lwcf/outdoor-recreation-legacy-partnership-grants-program.htm; U.S. Department of the Interior, "Interior

Department announces nearly $22 million for local parks and new actions to increase outdoor access in urban areas," (December 17, 2023 2023), https://www.doi.gov/pressreleases/interior-department-announces-nearly-22-million-local-parks-and-new-actions-increase.

55 Nohely T. Alvarez, Bi'Anncha T. Andrews, and Willow S. Lung-Amam, "Small Business Anti-Displacement Toolkit: A Guide for Small Business Leaders," *Small Business Anti-Displacement Network, University of Maryland* (2021); Levy, Comey, and Padilla, "In the face of gentrification."

56 Rigolon and Christensen, *Greening without Gentrification: Learning from Parks-Related Anti-displacement Strategies Nationwide.*

57 Rigolon et al., "More than 'Just Green Enough.'"

58 California State Parks, "Office of Community Involvement," (n.d.), https://www.parks.ca.gov/?page_id=24510; KangJae Jerry Lee, Jonathan Casper, and Myron Floyd, "Racial and ethnic diversity and inclusion efforts of public park and recreation agencies," *Journal of Park and Recreation Administration* 38, no. 1 (2020); Marsha Mercer, "State Parks Are Trying to Attract More Diverse Visitors," *Stateline* (MAY 31, 2022). https://stateline.org/2022/05/31/state-parks-are-trying-to-attract-more-diverse-visitors/#:~:text=Since%202020%2C%20more%20state%20park,they%20will%20feel%20more%20comfortable.

59 Patricia E. Salkin and Amy Lavine, "Understanding community benefits agreements: Equitable development, social justice and other considerations for developers, municipalities and community organizations," *The UCLA Journal of Environmental Law & Policy* 26 (2008); Laura Wolf-Powers, "Community benefits agreements and local government: A review of recent evidence," *Journal of the American Planning Association* 76, no. 2 (2010).

60 Bridget A. Vance, "A Winning Strategy for Community Equity in Detroit: Is a Community Benefits Ordinance the Most Effective Approach," *Wayne Law Review* 63, no. 3 (2018).

61 Wolf-Powers, "Community benefits agreements and local government."

62 Vance, "A Winning Strategy for Community Equity in Detroit," 770.

63 Arjen Buijs et al., "Mosaic governance for urban green infrastructure: Upscaling active citizenship from a local government perspective," *Urban Forestry & Urban Greening* 40 (2019); Vera Ferreira et al., "Stakeholders' engagement on nature-based solutions: A systematic literature review," *Sustainability* 12, no. 2 (2020).

64 Victoria Campbell-Arvai and Mark Lindquist, "From the ground up: Using structured community engagement to identify objectives for urban green infrastructure planning," *Urban Forestry & Urban Greening* 59 (2021); Lauren E. Mullenbach et al., "An antiracist, anticolonial agenda for urban greening and conservation," *Conservation Letters* 15, no. 4 (2022); Jeff Rose et al., "Incorporating Movements for Racial Justice into Planning and Management of US National Parks," *Journal of Park & Recreation Administration* 40, no. 1 (2022); Christoph D.D. Rupprecht and Jason A. Byrne, "Informal urban greenspace: comparison of quantity and characteristics in Brisbane, Australia and Sapporo, Japan," *PloS one* 9, no. 6 (2014).

65 Emilia Oscilowicz et al., "Grassroots mobilization for a just, green urban future: Building community infrastructure against green gentrification and displacement," *Journal of Urban Affairs* (2023); Taya Lynn Triffo, "Green infrastructure planning in Vancouver: addressing environmental justice with participatory resident workshops" (University of British Columbia, 2022).

66 Triffo, "Green infrastructure planning in Vancouver."; Tracy E. Perkins, *Evolution of a Movement: Four Decades of California Environmental Justice Activism* (University of California Press, 2022).

67 Isabelle Anguelovski, "Tactical developments for achieving just and sustainable neighborhoods: The role of community-based coalitions and bottom-to-bottom networks in street, technical, and funder activism," *Environment and Planning C: Government and Policy* 33, no. 4 (2015); Oscilowicz et al., "Grassroots mobilization for a just, green urban future."

68 Buijs et al., "Mosaic governance for urban green infrastructure"; Winifred Curran and Trina Hamilton, "Just green enough: Contesting environmental gentrification in Greenpoint, Brooklyn," *Local Environment* 17, no. 9 (2012); Alessandro Rigolon and Jeremy Németh, "'We're not in the business of housing': Environmental gentrification and the nonprofitization of green infrastructure projects," *Cities* 81 (2018), https://doi.org/10.1016/j.cities.2018.03.016.

69 Ferreira et al., "Stakeholders' engagement on nature-based solutions."; Alexander PN van der Jagt et al., "With the process comes the progress: A systematic review to support governance assessment of urban nature-based solutions," *Urban Forestry & Urban Greening* (2023); Helen Toxopeus et al., "How 'just' is hybrid governance of urban nature-based solutions?" *Cities* 105 (2020).

70 Sitong Luo and Agnès Patuano, "Multiple ecosystem services of informal green spaces: A literature review," *Urban Forestry & Urban Greening* 81 (2023); Rupprecht and Byrne, "Informal urban green-space"; Daria Sikorska et al., "The role of informal green spaces in reducing inequalities in urban green space availability to children and seniors," *Environmental science & policy* 108 (2020).

71 Troy D. Glover, Diana C. Parry, and Kimberly J. Shinew, "Building relationships, accessing resources: Mobilizing social capital in community garden contexts," *Journal of Leisure Research* 37, no. 4 (2005); Isaac Middle et al., "Integrating community gardens into public parks: An innovative approach for providing ecosystem services in urban areas," *Urban Forestry & Urban Greening* 13, no. 4 (2014); Rob Porter and Heather McIlvaine-Newsad, "Gardening in green space for environmental justice: Food security, leisure and social capital," *Leisure/Loisir* 37, no. 4 (2013).

72 "By the Numbers," National Park Service n.d., Retrieved on April 19, 2024 from https://www.nps.gov/articles/000/by-the-numbers.htm#:~:text=The%20NPS%20has%20about%2018,percent%20and%2013.4%20percent%2C%20respectively.

73 U.S. Bureau of Labor Statistics, "Employed persons by detailed industry, sex, race, and Hispanic or Latino ethnicity," (2022). https://www.bls.gov/cps/cpsaat18.htm.

74 Sammie L. Powers, Nicholas A. Pitas, and Andrew J. Mowen, "Critical Consciousness of Systemic Racism in Parks among Park Agency Directors and Policymakers: An Environmental Justice Tool for Recreation and Conservation Leaders," *Society & Natural Resources* 37, no. 1 (2024).

75 Lee, Casper, and Floyd, "Racial and ethnic diversity and inclusion efforts"; Mercer, "State Parks Are Trying to Attract More Diverse Visitors."; Courtney L. Schultz et al., "Whose National Park Service? An Examination of Relevancy, Diversity, and Inclusion Programs from 2005–2016," *Journal of Park and Recreation Administration* (2019).

76 Rasul A. Mowatt et al., "'Embarrassingly white' faculty racial disparities in American recreation, park, and tourism programs," *Schole: A Journal of Leisure Studies and Recreation Education* 31, no. 1 (2016): 37.

77 Terry L. Sharik et al., "Undergraduate enrollment in natural resource programs in the United States: Trends, drivers, and implications for the future of natural resource professions," *Journal of Forestry* 113, no. 6 (2015).
78 KangJae Jerry Lee, "The myth of African American under-representation in nature tourism," *Tourism Geographies* (2023).
79 Rosenzweig and Blackmar, *The park and the people*, chapter 12; Taylor, "Central Park as a model for social control."
80 Colin Fisher, "Multicultural Wilderness: Immigrants, African Americans, and Industrial Workers in the Forest Preserves and Dunes of Jazz-Age Chicago," *Environmental Humanities* 12, no. 1 (2020).
81 McCammack, *Landscapes of Hope*.
82 Gary A. O'Dell, "The Celebrated Black Explorer Stephen Bishop and Mammoth Cave: Observations by an English Journalist in 1853," *National Speleological Society* 76, no. 9 (2018); "African American History," National Park Service, n.d., Retrieved on June 1, 2024 from https://www.nps.gov/maca/learn/historyculture/african-american-history.htm.
83 Katie Algeo, "Underground tourists/tourists underground: African American tourism to Mammoth Cave," *Tourism Geographies* 15, no. 3 (2013).
84 Kathy S. Mason, "Buffalo Soldiers as Guardians of the Parks: African-American Troops in the California National Parks in the Early Twentieth Century," *The Historian* 81, no. 1 (2019).
85 Terence Young, "'A Contradiction in Democratic Government': WJ Trent, Jr., and the Struggle to Desegregate National Park Campgrounds," *Environmental History* 14, no. 4 (2009).
86 The Southern Poverty Law Center, "SPLC reports over 160 confederate symbols removed in 2020," (February 23, 2021), https://www.splcenter.org/presscenter/splc-reports-over-160-confederate-symbols-removed-2020.
87 Rose et al., "Incorporating Movements for Racial Justice."
88 Baird, "1916 Confederate Soldiers' Memorial Fountain."
89 Christina Simko, David Cunningham, and Nicole Fox, "Contesting commemorative landscapes: Confederate monuments and trajectories of change," *Social problems* 69, no. 3 (2022).
90 "Robert E. Lee Park," The Historical Marker Database 2020, accessed April 15, 2024, https://www.hmdb.org/m.asp?m=149087; NBCDFW, "Former Lee Park in Dallas Renamed Turtle Creek Park," (2019). https://www.nbcdfw.com/news/local/former-lee-park-in-dallas-renamed-turtle-creek-park/250830/.
91 Ashley Kairis, "Town Manager's Report: Knights Request Columbus' Return," *CaryCitizen.NEWS* (July 13, 2020), https://carycitizen.news/2020/07/13/harolds-blog-mask-extension-columbus-monument-removed-and-more/.
92 P.H. Gobster, "Managing urban parks for a racially and ethnically diverse clientele," *Leisure Sciences* 24, no. 2 (2002); Lena Le, "Hispanic and white visitors in US national parks: Meta-analysis of visitor use survey," *Journal of Park and Recreation Administration* 30, no. 4 (2012); Howard E.A. Tinsley, Diane J. Tinsley, and Chelsey E. Croskeys, "Park usage, social milieu, and psychosocial benefits of park use reported by older urban park users from four ethnic groups," *Leisure sciences* 24, no. 2 (2002); Jason W. Whiting et al., "Outdoor recreation motivation and site preferences across diverse racial/ethnic groups: A case study of Georgia state parks," *Journal of Outdoor Recreation and Tourism* 18 (2017).

93 Pinckney et al., "'We have our own cultural ways of being in nature'"; Aby Sene-Harper, Rasul A. Mowatt, and Myron F. Floyd, "A people's future of leisure studies: Political cultural black outdoors experiences," *Journal of Park and Recreation Administration* 40, no. 1 (2022).
94 Jonathan E. Vespa, Lauren Medina, and David M. Armstrong, "Demographic turning points for the United States: Population projections for 2020 to 2060," no. P25-1144 (2018).
95 Slippers-N-Sliders Ski Club, (n.d.), https://slippers-n-sliders.org/about-us/.
96 Jonathan J. Fisk et al., "Cultivating sovereignty in parks and protected areas: Sowing the seeds of restorative and transformative justice through the# LANDBACK movement" (paper presented at the Parks Stewardship Forum, 2021).
97 Audrey Glendenning, Martin Nie, and Monte Mills, "(Some) Land Back... Sort of: The Transfer of Federal Public Lands to Indian Tribes since 1970," *Natural Resources Journal* 63, no. 2 (2023); Sierra Kennedy, "This land is not our land, this land is their land: returning National Park Lands to their rightful protectors," *American Indian Law Journal* 10, no. 1 (2022).
98 Vanessa Racehorse and Anna Hohag, "Achieving Climate Justice Through Land Back: An Overview of Tribal Dispossession, Land Return Efforts, and Practical Mechanisms for #LandBack," *Colorado Environmental Law Journal* 34, no. 2 (2023); Brett G. Roberts, "Returning the Land: Native Americans and National Parks," *Ave Maria Law Review* 21 (2023).
99 Kevin K. Washburn, "Facilitating tribal co-management of federal public lands," *Wisconsin Law Review* 2 (2022): 266.
100 Kennedy, "This land is not our land, this land is their land"; Washburn, "Facilitating tribal co-management of federal public lands."
101 M. Kat Anderson and Michael G. Barbour, "Simulated indigenous management: a new model for ecological restoration in national parks," *Ecological Restoration* 21, no. 4 (2003); Fisk et al., "Cultivating sovereignty in parks and protected areas."
102 Racehorse and Hohag, "Achieving Climate Justice Through Land Back."
103 Frederick Douglass, *Two Speeches by Frederick Douglass* (Rochester, NY: 1857), http://www.libraryweb.org/~digitized/books/Two_Speeches_by_Frederick_Douglass.pdf.
104 Frederick Douglass, *Narrative of the Life of Frederick Douglass, an American Slave* (Anti-slavery Office, 1845).

5 Creating Democratic Parks in an Undemocratic Nation?

Perhaps the most important thing I learned was about democracy, that democracy is not our government, our constitution, our legal structure. Too often they are enemies of democracy.
    Howard Zinn, in reference to his experience of participating
    in the racial justice movement during the 1950s and 60s[1]

What is democracy exactly? Democracy has been the core justification of American public parks since their inception. Moreover, democracy was the founding ideology of the United States of America. However, distinguished historian Howard Zinn pointedly notes that the very structures that support the United States, its government, constitution, and legal systems, often act as "enemies" of democracy. This chapter explores this poignant contradiction and its relevance to the present and future of American public parks.

Various forms of democracy have been practiced in human societies over the past 250 years. In broad strokes, democracy entails a governmental system and political process in which all citizens can freely and equally participate in state affairs. Thus, freedom and equality are two central elements of democracy: Citizens have the freedom to express, support, and mobilize certain political views without fear of reprisal, and they have equal rights to participate in political decision-making and electoral processes. Without these elements, democracy would be in jeopardy.[2]

In the context of public parks, then, the freedom and equality associated with democracy can be manifested in two specific ways. First, as asserted by many park creators, everyone has unrestricted, free access to parks. Second, everyone has freedom and equal opportunity to participate in park planning and management decisions. As we witnessed from previous chapters, neither of these ideals has been fully realized due to systemic park injustice. Despite the people's struggle to make public parks more democratic spaces, parks are not evenly distributed across American communities, and decision-making in park planning and management remains predominantly elitist, top-down, deceitful, and capitalistic. Additionally, high entrance fees and reservation

DOI: 10.4324/9781032707624-8

systems, often justified for crowd control and environmental protection, further preclude "free and equal" access to parks.[3]

How then can we eradicate systemic park injustice and make public parks truly democratic spaces? As detailed in the previous chapter, people have developed counterstrategies to cope with systemic park injustice. Yet, those efforts usually remain at the micro- and meso-levels, falling short of interrogating the broader, macro-level contexts that gave rise to the park injustice. In this final chapter, I advocate for a more comprehensive analysis that directly confronts the colonialism, capitalism, elitism, racism, and sexism of the White ruling class. A critical examination of these "-isms" that have shaped U.S. history is imperative because these same forces shaped the country's public parks. Put differently, it was highly unlikely that public parks could ever function as democratic spaces because they have been nested in an undemocratic, if not, an anti-democratic U.S. society. Systemic park injustice is not the issue limited to the parks themselves, but one of many social injustices that germinated from an unjust American society. In this regard, American public parks epitomize some of the ugliest aspects of American society.

This chapter aims to build upon the previous chapter and extend our fight against systemic park injustice onto a broader battleground. By linking historical injustices perpetuated in public parks to those in American society at large, we will be able to better understand and strategize for a more just future. Below, I first offer a succinct review of the colonial and capitalist roots of the U.S. and then expand my critical lens to the elitism, sexism, and racism of elite White men. It is essential to recognize that these "-isms" do not operate in isolation. Rather, they are deeply intertwined with one another and mutually constitutive in creating cultural and material realities that benefit the White ruling class. Addressing this web of oppressive ideologies is indispensable for charting paths toward a more democratic future—for both American public parks and American society.

Colonialism and Capitalism

To understand the origin of systemic park injustice, we must examine its inextricable link with colonialism and capitalism. Colonialism seeks economic benefits by establishing colonies in other countries or societies through military conquest and political domination.[4] Beginning from Christopher Columbus's discovery of the New World in 1497, European colonists completely disregarded Indigenous sovereignties, robbed their lands, enslaved Indigenous peoples, and extracted valuable resources.[5] The bloody colonial conquest in the Americas was justified by the Doctrine of Discovery, which prominent historian Roxanne Dunbar-Ortiz pointedly summarizes as a "legal cover for theft."[6] The Doctrine is an international law developed in the 15th and 16th centuries by England, Spain, Portugal, and the Church, stipulating that European monarchs can claim ownership rights over any lands outside of Europe inhabited by non-Christians.[7] Millions of Indigenous peoples in the Americas perished due to European colonialism.

When Colonial Americans broke up with Great Britain and established their own country, they did not abandon European colonial practices, but instead developed and practiced their own version of colonialism against Indigenous peoples. In 1792, Thomas Jefferson embraced the Doctrine of Discovery and claimed that it was international law applicable to the new U.S. government. Similarly, in the *1823 Johnson v. McIntosh* case, the U.S. Supreme Court cited the Doctrine as a well-established international law, ruling that Indigenous peoples could not own land, because it belonged to the U.S. government.[8] It is an irony that gets lost in sanitized versions of history: White Americans fought against British colonial control, but they fully embraced colonialism against Indigenous peoples.

American colonial enterprise continued during the 20th century and is *still in force* today. From the 19th to 20th centuries, the U.S. government acquired or annexed the lands of Mexico, Alaska, Puerto Rico, Guam, the Philippines, Cuba, American Samoa, the Marshall Islands, the Northern Mariana Islands, and Hawaii.[9] In the 21st century, American colonial and imperial ideologies have been manifested through the massive U.S. defense budget and extensive military operations across the globe.[10] For example, the Iraq War in 2003 was not really about democracy or the "war on terrorism," but was instead primarily motivated by the Bush administration's desire to control oil resources and maintain American global hegemony.[11] In his critique of American colonial and imperial foreign policy, Kaplan concluded that "people hundreds of years from now will look back on the United States at the turn of the 21st century and have no problem calling it an American empire."[12]

Capitalism was another major social force that contributed to the birth of systemic park injustice. At the time of European colonial invasions of the Americas, Europe was under a feudal system where powerful monarchies and lords ruled the peasants and serfs. Class mobility was limited, because one's status was based on heredity. As the immense scale of European colonial conquest progressed in the Americas and Africa during the 15th to the 17th centuries, so did the influx of an unprecedented amount of capital to Europe. Gradually, some merchants, traders, bankers, and lawyers accumulated an enormous amount of capital, and they used it to dismantle the feudal system and seize power from monarchies and lords, creating a new economic and political order based on private property ownership and capital accumulation.[13]

The economic and political system of British colonies in America diverged from feudalism and was more in line with capitalism as the colonists were able to own lands and there was no hereditary nobility. The development of modern capitalism in the New World, marked by exploitative class struggles between the wealthy and the poor, was predicable: From the onset, the colonial invasion of the Americas was all about capital accumulation.[14] The rich merchants exploited the working-class with minimal wages and harsh treatment, and class conflicts frequently erupted in Colonial America. To address labor shortages, English colonists not only enslaved Indigenous peoples but also brought indentured servants, contract laborers from Europe. Over half of the colonists who came to North America during the colonial period came as servants, and many of them died during their journey to the New World. Surviving servants faced abuse from their masters. Beating, whipping, and raping of servants was common. Chronic starvation and famine, deadly diseases, and frequent Indian attacks only worsened the misery. Many servants died or committed suicide.[15]

Enslaved Indigenous peoples and indentured servants were gradually replaced by enslaved Africans. Europeans and Colonial Americans held racial prejudice that Africans were stronger than Indigenous people—a more effective solution to chronic labor shortage.[16] By 1800, Dutch, English, French, Portuguese, and Danish Europeans transported 10 to 15 million Africans as slaves to the Americas.[17] Colonial America evolved into an aristocratic and tyrannical society based on capital accumulation, laying the foundation of the United States of America. Today, U.S. society has become what Feagin and Ducey astutely note as an oligopolistic capitalist society where a small group of extremely wealthy White men dominate the national economy.[18]

Thus, both colonialism and capitalism created fertile ground for violent, oppressive, and exploitative social systems and practices, such as systemic park injustice, to germinate in the U.S. By the time American public parks began to emerge in the mid-19th century, colonial and capitalist ideologies had deeply woven into the economic and political fabrics of the U.S., creating explicit class and racial hierarchies. Within such a social structure of American society, public parks were well-poised to serve the interests of the ruling class at the expense of vulnerable and marginalized groups. Given this broader historical context of the U.S., the emergence of systemic park injustice was only a natural consequence.

Today, colonialism and capitalism continue to shape the everyday reality of American society and its public parks. Many researchers point out that the colonial dimension of public parks is evident in spatial dispossession and park gentrification that disproportionately harm racial and ethnic minorities and the poor.[19] Perhaps the most recent and representative example of spatial dispossession in parks is the Supreme Court decision on the *City of Grants Pass v. Johnson case* in June 2024. The background of this landmark case is that, because of an increasing number of people experiencing homelessness, the City of Grants Pass, Oregon has implemented several local ordinances prohibiting people from camping and sleeping in public spaces, including parks. In 2018, a class action lawsuit against the city was filed on behalf of Debra Black, a person experiencing homelessness. In 2020, Oregon District Court ruled that the city violated the Ninth Circuit's precedent in *Martin v. Boise* and the Eighth Amendment's Excessive Fines Clause because the city did not have sufficient shelter houses. Black passed away in 2021, yet Gloria Johnson and John Logan were assigned as the class representatives for the city's subsequent appeals to the Ninth Circuit Court, and eventually the U.S. Supreme Court. On the 28th June 2024, the Supreme Court ruled in a 6–3 decision that cities can enforce bans on people sleeping outside even when they have nowhere else to go. The Court also emphasized that homelessness is a complex issue and federal judges do not have the authority to dictate cities' policies. Subsequently, many cities and civil rights organizations argued that the decision deteriorated American democracy, because it created a legal ground for criminalizing the life-sustaining activities of one of the most vulnerable groups.[20]

Similarly, the capitalist dimension of public parks is easily identifiable from the influx of large private funds in new park planning as well as the creation of commercial stores. These two trends in public parks represent capitalists' strategic search for profit. Within the capitalist growth ideology, new parks must be bigger and fancier, in keeping with the completed or ongoing park projects in major cities previously mentioned in this book. The encroachment of capitalist ideologies is gradually eroding public parks' democratic ideals and transforming them into a space of consumption and commerce.[21]

Elitism, Racism, and Sexism of Elite White Men

The colonial and capitalist ideologies ingrained in American history have intimately dovetailed with the enduring elitism, racism, and sexism of the White ruling class, creating cultural and material realities that make it extremely difficult to establish democratic public parks. Again, this troubling history can be traced back to the very beginning of the United States of America. Dunbar-Ortiz acutely states that "all modern nation-states claim a kind of rationalized origin story upon which they fashion patriotism or loyalty to the state." Similarly, Loewen criticizes that American history textbooks are riddled with distortions and omissions to emphasize American exceptionalism. Relatedly, even though democracy, liberty, justice, and equality are considered the core justifications of the Revolutionary War and, subsequently, the founding values of the United States of America, overwhelming historical evidence suggests otherwise.[22]

The Revolutionary War was not a crusade for a democratic and independent nation, but a tactical response from the dominant class in Colonial America to solidify their privileged social status. The War could provide two distinctive benefits to the ruling class: (1) Economic gain from taking over land, profit, and the tax system from England and (2) Containing rebellions from Indigenous peoples, poor Whites, and enslaved Africans who frequently sought to overthrow the ruling class. When the idea of independence started to emerge in Colonial America, the majority of people had little to no interest in it. It certainly had no appeal to Indigenous and Black people. Here, the elite White men enticed the poor Whites with an opportunity to change their social status through the ranking and monetary rewards attached to military service. The ruling class mobilized the lower class by using the rewards and the language of liberty and equality, successfully diverting the rebellious energy of the masses to the British Empire. The war was orchestrated by elite White men and executed by ordinary and poor people.[23]

The circumstances surrounding the creation of two foundational documents of the U.S., the Declaration of Independence and the Constitution of the United States of America, provide a further glimpse into how deeply elitism, racism, and sexism are embedded in American society. At the time Thomas Jefferson drafted the Declaration which states "all men are created equal," he enslaved 180 Black people. The Declaration also describes Indigenous peoples as "the merciless Indian Savages, whose known rule of warfare, is an undistinguished destruction of all ages, sexes and conditions."[24] The 55 founding fathers who drafted and signed the U.S. Constitution were all White men with considerable wealth, and about 45% of them owned slaves in their lifetimes, and many of them profited from slave trading businesses. There were no "founding mothers" because no women were included in the Constitutional Convention. In fact, all the personal properties and income of women were legally owned by their husbands. No Indigenous peoples, Blacks, and White servants participated in the Convention. Property ownership and slavery were the two subjects the founding fathers discussed the most when drafting the Constitution, because they had to protect what they possessed.[25] Zinn summarized the Constitution this way:

> When economic interest is seen behind the political clauses of the Constitution, then the document becomes not simply the work of wise men trying to establish a decent and orderly society, but the work of certain groups trying to maintain their privileges, while giving just enough rights and liberties to enough of the people to ensure popular support.[26]

The newly formed nation retained its colonial roots. The only people who were allowed to vote for political leaders were White men of wealth and property. Limited voting rights made it nearly impossible for women, Indigenous peoples, Blacks, and poor Whites to engage in political activity, severely undermining the democracy, liberty, justice, and equality promised in the Declaration and the Constitution. Women did not gain full suffrage until the 19th Amendment in 1920. For people of color, the Voting Rights Act of 1965 finally prohibited racial discrimination in voting. It took nearly 200 years to ensure equal voting rights in the U.S.[27]

Elitism, racism, and sexism still linger in the U.S. today. American elites remain overwhelmingly affluent White men, dominating major U.S. economic, political, educational, and media institutions since the founding of the country.[28] No woman has ever been U.S. president in its 250 years of history, and studies have shown that, for decades, the average annual income of women is several thousand dollars less than that of men, even though the two groups have the same education level.[29] Systemic racism continues to threaten the lives and well-being of people of color, and it permeates virtually every facet of American society, including its criminal justice system, education, employment, entertainment, healthcare, housing, media, and politics.[30]

No wonder systemic park injustice emerged from this historically elitist, racist, and sexist society. How could we expect parks to be anything different? The beginnings of the U.S. nationhood and American public parks show striking similarities, and in fact, they run in almost parallel histories. In both cases, the dominant class promised democracy, justice, and liberty to the subordinate class, but the former seldom delivered them. As we witnessed in the previous chapters, public parks were built and managed by elite White men to materialize their interests while deceiving, exploiting, displacing, and even murdering people with limited means and power. Sexist ideologies permeated public parks and the American conservation movement, and some outdoor recreation activities, such as fishing and hunting, are still male-dominated.[31] Eugenics and White supremacy undergirded the creation of public parks, and racial discrimination has long curtailed people of color from enjoying public parks. The classed, racialized, and gendered nature of American public parks is not at all surprising given the enduring elitism, racism, and sexism in the U.S.

Toward Democratic American Public Parks

My analysis thus far indicates that systemic park injustice is an outgrowth of the undemocratic or anti-democratic American society. Recognizing this intrinsic connection between park injustice and enduring colonialism, capitalism, elitism, racism, and sexism in the U.S., it is evident that democratic public parks are unlikely to be accomplished if the current systems remain intact. It means that, along with micro- and meso-level strategies summarized in the previous chapter, we need macro-level changes in American society to bring about democratic public parks. But how?

Significantly, more than a century ago, German philosopher Karl Marx illustrated a pathway to a more democratic society. Through his incisive analysis on capitalism, Marx has made a profound intellectual impact across a wide range of academic disciplines and inspired revolutionary changes in the economic and political systems of various countries. In his writings, Marx argued that it is impossible to establish a democratic government in a capitalist society, because capitalism is inherently exploitative and hierarchical.[32]

Marx explained that capitalism, like feudalism and slavery, creates an unequal class structure, the social division between the bourgeoisie, a small group of people who own and control the means of production and appropriation of the profit (or surplus, in Marxist terms) and the proletariat, the subordinate majority hired by the bourgeoisie to generate profits. The power imbalance between the two groups is evident, and their relationship is predisposed to conflict. Since the bourgeoisie compete for more profits, they always seek to maximize capital accumulation by cutting production costs such as lowering employee wages and replacing the laborers with an automized production system. The proletariat have no control over the production or appropriation of surpluses, but they must receive a fair wage from the bourgeoisie and compete among themselves. In this hierarchical and exploitative class structure which induces suffering and degradation of the majority, democracy is, in Marx's view, impossible to obtain.[33]

Furthermore, Marx believed that capitalism is inescapably a contradictory and unsustainable system. For example, the state, or the government, within a capitalistic system, is dependent on the material resources that the system creates. Hence, if the state intervenes in the exploitative practice of the bourgeoisie, it inevitably undermines the process of capital accumulation, which in turn compromises the state's material foundation.[34] Moreover, when capitalists attempt to generate greater capital accumulation by lowering wages or replacing workers with machines, it negatively affects the workers' purchasing power, which in turn diminishes capitalists' profit-making because the workers cannot purchase and consume capitalists' products. This paradoxical situation drives capitalists to expand and intensify their exploitative methods even further, creating a vicious cycle in which they have to continuously escalate labor exploitation against the majority as well as resource extraction from finite natural resources.[35] Capitalists always want more, not solely because they are greedy but because the capitalist system undermines their overall success.[36]

Recognizing capitalism as a suicidal and self-destructive economic and political system, Marx envisioned transition from capitalism to *socialism*, and eventually *communism*, as a viable pathway to a more democratic society. It must be first noted that socialism and communism have been poorly understood and taught by generations of Americans, partly due to McCarthyism and the systematic anti-communist campaign during the Cold War era. Marx's idea of socialism and communism has nothing to do with the dictatorship, anarchism, or radicalism those anti-communism movements conjured, and many different types of socialism and communism have been developed and practiced since his time. In the Marxist tradition, the distinction between capitalism, socialism, and communism is primarily based on who owns and controls the means of production and the appropriation of surplus. Marx analyzed that, since capitalism is based on surplus and capital accumulation, a successful transition to a better society hinges on the elimination of private ownership and class structure. What he advocated using the terms socialism and communism (which he often used interchangeably) was a more collectivistic and communal society where the state owns and controls the production and the appropriation on behalf of its citizens.[37]

To make it work, he believed that the state must build full accountability and transparency to the majority by making all government personnel to be selected by frequent elections. Their elected positions could be revocable, bound by the instructions of their constituency. In so doing, the majority will maintain direct influence on state affairs, and power will be equally distributed. Moreover, Marx believed that, as this transition from capitalism to socialism progresses further, the state will reach communism, a highly unified society where everybody owns and manages the production and distribution collectively. Here, the government and laws no longer exist because the society is effectively self-regulated. The state and its constituents are fully integrated, so that one individual's pursuits of basic needs perfectly align with that of the society and the state. In summary, Marx believed that democracy can be accomplished by moving away from the hierarchical and individualistic social structure of capitalism to a more egalitarian and collectivistic social system accentuated by collective property ownership, decision-making, and governance. Through this transition, all individuals will be liberated from material needs and be able to freely pursue their own self-actualizations.[38]

Clearly, it is naïve to think that socialism will be an elixir to all the problems of capitalism in contemporary American society, or that the translation of socialism into specific laws, rules, and social orders could be easily done. Indeed, Marx noted that the transition to socialism would be a challenging and lengthy process, requiring collective and determined actions from the proletariat. Moreover, history has witnessed that Marx's ideas have been seriously misused or abused, such as the extreme totalitarian regime of Joseph Stalin in the Soviet Union and Pol Pot in Cambodia, resulting in the death and suffering of millions of innocent people.[39]

However, it is important to understand that Marx's socialist ideas have already been incorporated into the economic and political system of the U.S. In fact, capitalism, socialism, and communism are not independent of one another, but they comprise a continuum of economic and political systems based on the extent to which the state owns and controls the production and distribution of surplus. Thus, extreme capitalism at one end of the spectrum allows exclusive private property ownership, into which the state cannot interfere, under any circumstances. Extreme communism, at the other end of the spectrum, assumes absolute state ownership and control of all social sectors and properties. What this continuum indicates is that our decision for economic and political systems should not be, or cannot be, based on which one to choose among the three. Rather, it should be about the ratio—that is, about how much of each we will adopt. Capitalism, socialism, and communism have always co-existed.

Indeed, many existing national economies have historically used a mixture of these economic systems, and the U.S. is no exception. During the 1930s, for example, the Great Depression brought millions of industrial workers to a federation of unions called The Congress of Industrial Organizations (CIO). The CIO allied with the U.S. Democratic Party and Communist Party and together, they demanded large corporations and politicians provide more jobs and better living conditions. Their collective effort made President Franklin D. Roosevelt initiate new and innovative programs, which distinguished Marxian economist Richard Wolff describes as the following:

In short, FDR's government taxed the rich more than ever before and used the money to provide mass public services more than ever before. FDR established the Social Security system, the first federal unemployment compensation system, the first federal minimum wage, and a mass federal jobs program, among other government-supported social programs.[40]

Notice that all of these socialist initiatives were aimed at fulfilling the basic needs of American citizens—a remarkably more democratic, progressive, and egalitarian approach than capitalist practices. However, after the death of FDR and the end of World War II, American socialists and communists' yearning for further democratic progress was crushed by the systematic anti-communism movement that private capitalists and the Republican Party orchestrated. At that time, both socialism and communism were treated as anti-American and serious threats to public safety. The U.S. government tracked down, arrested, imprisoned, and deported political leaders, blacklisted Hollywood actors and directors, and fired teachers and professors who expressed or supported socialist and communist thinking.[41]

Despite such a setback, Americans' desire to create a democratic society through socialism has gradually gained momentum over the past few decades. During the 2016 and 2020 presidential campaigns, for example, Bernie Sanders, a U.S. Senator from Vermont, emerged as the most popular and influential socialist. Self-identified as a "democratic socialist", Sanders' political agendas were social and economic equity and robust welfare systems such as universal healthcare, free college tuition, and higher taxation on the rich. He also emphasized grassroots movements for social reform, receiving enthusiastic support from younger, working-class, and racial and ethnic minority voters. His broad and strong voter support indicates that many Americans are fed up with capitalism and more accepting of socialism-based changes.[42] On the global scene, additionally, socialism-oriented countries such as Finland, Denmark, Iceland, Sweden, and Norway consistently rank among the happiest countries. In the 2024 World Happiness Report, the U.S. was ranked 23rd in the world for happiness, an embarrassingly low rank given its economic size.[43]

Socialism in Action: Democratic Workplace and Voting System

It may be hard to imagine how American society steeped in a strong capitalist tradition could adopt more socialist ideologies and practices, or how socialism might manifest in American public parks. In this section, I attempt to illustrate the ways in which socialism could promote democratic changes in the business sector and the U.S. voting system. Both of these cases have strong implications for public park management.

Democratic Workplaces

Wolff argues that socialist ideologies can bring about democratic changes in the business sector, which can be gradually extended into politics and other social realms. He highlights Workers' Self-Directed Enterprises (WSDE) and Worker Co-ops (WC) as specific examples.[44] According to Wolff, both WSDE and WC express a microeconomic transformation and socialist business model that depart from the archetypes of capitalist enterprises such as elitist, hierarchical, and exploitative relationships between workers, managers, the board of directors, and owners. In WSDE and WC, workers who produce the surpluses at their workplaces collectively decide how to appropriate and distribute those surpluses. Moreover, unlike Worker-Owned Enterprises or Worker-Managed Enterprises, WSDE and WC make their workers own the workplaces and function as owners and the board of directors, so that they have an equal voice on key business decisions such as production, appropriation, and distribution of surplus. The workers must agree on the rules for collective decisions as well as the system for adjusting disputes and disagreements. Wolff argues that the transition from the employer/employee relationship in private and state workplaces to an alternative worker co-op organization "establishes real democracy in the economic sphere," which in turn, "offers better prospects for socialists to revitalize demands and movements for parallel democracy in the political one."[45]

WSDE and WC might sound abstract and utopian, yet Wolff underscores that they have a long history on the global scene. As a concrete example, he cites Corporación Mondragón in the Basque region of Spain. The Mondragón Corporation was originally started by a young Catholic priest, José María Arizmendiarrieta in the 1940s as a vocational training school. Today, the organization has expanded into a group of more than 100 firms, and it is one of Spain's 10 largest corporations, with over 80,000 workers and €12.5 billion in annual revenue. Arizmendiarrieta's main vision was collective self-governance that respects the worker as person. In 1987, the Mondragón established ten basic principles such as free membership, democratic organization, sovereignty of labor, and self-management, to name a few. Mondragón has been seen as one of the most successful examples of democratic decision-making and worker-ownership in the business sector. Yet, critics note that the reality of Mondragón was far more bureaucratic, and one of its firms filed for bankruptcy in 2013.[46] Still, other researchers believed that Mondragón's continuing success demonstrated how worker co-ops can thrive alongside capitalist workplaces, offering effective strategies for democratic work relationships.[47]

Notably, Mondragón's principles and their democratic vision overlap with some of the counterstrategies mentioned in the previous chapter and the emerging trend in public park management. For example, both Community Participation (counterstrategy #5) and the co-management of national parks with Indigenous groups (counterstrategy #13) certainly align with the collective management and decision-making emphasized in the Mondragón principles. Moreover, Cascina Falchera, a multifunction property located outside of the city of Turin in Italy, exhibits some similarities with the central characteristics of WSDE and WC. Technically, Cascina Falchera is not a public park but "a common good of the city of Turin granted to the Kairòs Consortium, until 2040...with the aim of enhancing its educational vocation and transforming it into a hub of social innovation."[48] Common goods are owned by the state yet managed jointly by community members. Thus, they are different from public goods, or most public parks, that are owned and managed by the state for the public. Under this unique arrangement, Cascina Falchera is managed by the local citizens using public funds and the revenue generated from its agriculture, workshops, and events. Its citizen-driven, collective management approach has a strong socialist spirit that can inform American public parks.[49]

Democratic Voting System

In addition to the business sector, socialist principles and their democratic aspiration can inform changes in the U.S. voting system. Since the U.S. political system was built on elitist, sexist, and racist ideologies, its voting system is mainly designed to preserve the political dominance of elite White men. I argue that the U.S. Electoral College is the epitome of the undemocratic political system that needs immediate elimination.

The Electoral College is a complex voting mechanism established by the U.S. Constitution for the sole purpose of electing the president. Today, the system involves voters in each state casting ballots for a slate of electors pledged to their preferred presidential candidate. Each state has several electors equal to its total number of Senators and Representatives. In 48 states and Washington, D.C., the candidate who wins the majority of votes receives all its electoral votes. Exceptions to this "winner-take-all" system are Maine and Nebraska assigning the electors using a proportional system. A majority of 270 out of 538 total electoral votes is required to win the presidency. Thus, the system makes American citizens unable to vote for the president *directly*, and the "winner-take-all" system wastes the votes from large segments of the population. It also means that the Electoral College can make a candidate win the presidency without winning the national popular vote. Indeed, the system has elected the loser of the popular vote in five instances in U.S. history; 1876, 1888, 1960, 2000, and 2016.[50]

Prominent legal researchers and political scientists acutely noted that the Electoral College was a poorly designed system born out of a lengthy and tiring negotiation process among the founding fathers who had remarkably different interests and opinions. Indeed, the framers deliberated on the method of selecting the president for 22 days during the Constitutional Convention and had 30 votes to decide its specifics.[51] Robert A. Dahl concludes that the creation of the Electoral College was a "group of baffled and confused men who finally settle[d] on a solution more out of desperation than confidence. As events were soon to show, they had little understanding of how their solution would work out in practice."[52]

The Electoral College's undemocratic and flawed foundations are particularly evident in the two main issues that the framers debated and negotiated: Slavery and voter parochialism. Slavery was the greatest division between the Northern and Southern states and one of the main reasons that the framers chose the Electoral College over the popular vote. Some delegates opposed direct election of the president because it would be disadvantageous to the South due to their large slave population with no voting rights. To protect the South's interest, a compromise was made that Southern states could count three out of every five enslaved persons for the state's total population when calculating the number of the House of Representatives. Moreover, most delegates opposed direct election because they did not believe that citizens were capable of making a reasoned and informed decision on selecting the candidate. Although some delegates such as James Madison and Benjamin Franklin disagreed, the parochialism sentiment eventually prevailed.[53] To date, many attempts have been made to reform or abandon the Electoral College, yet none of them turned out to be successful for various reasons.[54] The Electoral College is a flawed system created nearly 250 years ago, but it is still in operation. It continues to prevent Americans' equal and fair participation in presidential elections, functioning as a major roadblock to a more democratic nation.

Violent and Verdant: A Crossroads

> ...all progress in capitalistic agriculture is a progress in the art, not only of robbing the labourer, but of robbing the soil; all progress in increasing the fertility of the soil for a given time, is a progress towards ruining the lasting sources of that fertility.
>
> Karl Marx[55]

When I visit public parks in the U.S., I often find myself reflecting on their violent history that starkly contrasts with the verdant scenes before me. People were abused, exploited, deceived, and even killed because of public parks, but parks continue to be one of the most beloved and coveted geographies in the nation. American public parks are indeed full of ironies and paradoxes. But what will be the future of these parks?

The more I pondered, the gloomier I became. Capitalism and its growth ideology have posed one of the greatest threats not only to public parks but to the entirety of humanity: *Climate change*.[56] Climate change has spurred extreme weather events, sea level rise, and ecosystem disruption. The World Meteorological Organization reported that 2023 was the hottest year in the 174-year record, and it is predicted that Earth's temperature will continue to rise in the following years.[57] Fossil fuel extraction by powerful oil and gas corporations, carbon dioxide emissions from automobiles and airplanes, deforestation from large mining and timbering operations, and methane emissions from livestock are all pushing Mother Earth to the brink.[58] Our very existence is at risk: One source estimated that high temperatures resulted in approximately 12,000 annual premature deaths in the contiguous U.S. during the 2010s.[59] In 2024 alone, extreme climate disasters have claimed hundreds of lives worldwide, and this number continues to climb at the time of this writing.[60]

These grave circumstances cast a long shadow over public parks. Basic economics tells us that scarcity increases value. Parks will be increasingly scarce as climate change continues to destroy the Earth's ecosystems. But parks will become more valuable to human beings because of their environmental and health benefits: providing plant and animal habitat, promoting biodiversity, and mitigating floods and heat island. It means that people will seek parks even more as they disappear. This is alarming because greater human use will only exacerbate parks' sustainability risks already posed by climate change.

In the short-term, more restrictions could be put in place to protect parks—higher entrance fees, limited reservations, stricter regulations and stronger enforcement, and temporary and seasonal closures. In fact, these managerial devices are already in place in a growing number of parks and other outdoor recreation areas. Yet, it is important to recognize that these are merely band-aid solutions because they do not address climate change, the fundamental cause of the park scarcity. With more restrictions, public parks become even harder to access, especially for vulnerable and marginalized community members.

With the compounding park scarcity and inaccessibility, what seems inevitable is greater competition. When competition for desirable resources intensifies, people are more likely to use their means and power to win. Especially worrisome here is that some people might abuse their means and power. As illustrated in the previous chapters, monopolization, exclusion, deception, privatization, and criminalization are all-too-familiar stories of systemic park injustice. What I see on the horizon is a continuation of this history of violence and oppression: Public parks that so many people have fought for democratic access will become increasingly inaccessible, disproportionately serving the privileged. Climate change is diminishing parks' identity as democratic public spaces. Public parks in the U.S. and elsewhere are poised to enter a new chapter of ugly history.

We are at a crossroads. Our next decision will determine not only the democracy of American public parks but the future of humanity. The current climate crisis urges us to engage in profound rethinking and philosophical reorientation regarding our ideas about social advancement and ways of living, ideas deeply rooted in capitalist growth model and discriminatory ideologies such as elitism, racism, and sexism. Capitalism, while providing material abundance, has done so at the cost of serious environmental destruction and human suffering.[61] Its growth ideology has been quietly killing us. It is time to wake up from capitalism's false promises of prosperity, material wealth, meritocracy, and comfortable living. Moreover, elitism, racism, and sexism tend to work in tandem with capitalism to exploit others. What do we gain by categorizing, ranking, and discriminating ourselves? It is time to end the history of hate and bigotry. We must redefine human progress and civilization based on fundamental human values such as love, empathy, liberty, and justice.

American public parks in the age of climate change serve as a powerful reminder that our fight for a better future must go on. Climate data have indicated that we are on the brink of an irreversible climate tipping point.[62] We must take action to prevent further environmental and human losses. At this critical juncture, we must think critically, and we must act decisively.

Notes

1 Howard Zinn, *You can't be neutral on a moving train: A personal history of our times* (Boston: Beacon Press, 2002), preface. p. x
2 See Robert A. Dahl, *On Democracy* (Yale University Press, 2020); Philippe C Schmitter and Terry Lynn Karl, "What democracy is… and is not," *Journal of Democracy* 2, no. 3 (1991); Larry Diamond and Leonardo Morlino, "The quality of democracy: An overview," *Journal of Democracy* 15, no. 4 (2004).
3 T.A. More, " 'The parks are being loved to death' and other frauds and deceits in recreation management," *Journal of Leisure Research* 34, no. 1 (2002): 53–56; Thomas More and Thomas Stevens, "Do user fees exclude low-income people from resource-based recreation?" *Journal of Leisure Research* 32, no. 3 (2000).
4 Ronald J. Horvath, "A definition of colonialism," *Current Anthropology* 13, no. 1 (1972).
5 John Grenier, *The First Way of War: American War Making on the Frontier, 1607–1814* (Cambridge University Press, 2005); Francis Jennings, "Virgin land and savage people," *American Quarterly* 23, no. 4 (1971); James W. Loewen, *Lies My Teacher Told Me: Everything Your American History Textbook Got Wrong* (The New Press, 2008).
6 Roxanne Dunbar-Ortiz, *An Indigenous Peoples' History of the United States* (Beacon Press, 2014), 198.
7 Robert J Miller et al., *Discovering Indigenous Lands: The Doctrine of Discovery in the English Colonies* (Oxford University Press, 2010).
8 Dunbar-Ortiz, *An Indigenous Peoples' History of the United States*, Chapter 11.
9 Dunbar-Ortiz, *An Indigenous Peoples' History of the United States*.
10 Robert D. Kaplan, *Imperial Grunts: On the Ground with the American Military, from Mongolia to the Philippines to Iraq and beyond* (Vintage Books, 2006).
11 Vassilis Fouskas and Bulent Gokay, *The New American Imperialism: Bush's War on Terror and Blood for Oil* (Bloomsbury Publishing USA, 2005).
12 Robert D. Kaplan, "America and the tragic limits of imperialism," *The Hedgehog Review* 5, no. 1 (2003), https://link.gale.com/apps/doc/A118678159/AONE?u=uofulawmain&sid=googleScholar&xid=9a9e7d16.
13 James M. Blaut, "Colonialism and the Rise of Capitalism," *Science & Society* 53, no. 3 (1989).
14 Blaut, "Colonialism and the Rise of Capitalism," 280; Jonathan Levy, *Ages of American Capitalism: A History of the United States* (Random House, 2021).
15 Howard Zinn, *A People's History of the United States* (HarperCollins, 2015), 46.
16 Ironically, one of the Europeans who opened the transatlantic slave trade between the Americas and Africa was Bartolomé de La Casas mentioned in Chapter 2. La Casas' intention was to alleviate the suffering of Indigenous people. For more information, see Ibram X. Kendi, *Stamped from the Beginning: The Definitive History of Racist Ideas in America* (Bold Type Books, 2016), 26–7.
17 Zinn, *A People's History of the United States*, 29.
18 Joe R. Feagin and Kimberley Ducey, *Elite White Men Ruling: Who, What, When, Where, and How* (Routledge, 2017).
19 Isabelle Anguelovski et al., "Decolonizing the green city: from environmental privilege to emancipatory green justice," *Environmental Justice* 15, no. 1

(2022); Emilia Lewartowska et al., "Racial Inequity in Green Infrastructure and Gentrtification: Challenging Compounded Environmental Racisms in the Green City," *International Journal of Urban and Regional Research* 48, no. 2 (2024); Sara Safransky, "Greening the urban frontier: Race, property, and resettlement in Detroit," *Geoforum* 56 (2014).

20 Hanna Rosin, "A Supreme Court Ruling on Homelessness That's Both Crucial and Useless: City of Grants Pass v. Johnson skips over the real issues," *The Atlantic* (2024, June 6), https://www.theatlantic.com/podcasts/archive/2024/06/homeless-supreme-court-case-grants-pass-johnson/678602/; Jeff Rose, "Unsheltered homelessness in urban parks: Perspectives on environment, health, and justice in Salt Lake City, Utah," *Environmental Justice* 12, no. 1 (2019); Jeff Rose, "Opinion: How a Supreme Court case will impact homelessness and democracy in Utah," *The Salt Lake Tribune* (2024, April 22), https://www.sltrib.com/opinion/commentary/2024/04/22/opinion-how-supreme-court-case/; Whitney K. Novak and Dave S. Sidhu, "The Eighth Amendment and homelessness: Supreme Court upholds camping ordinances in city of Grants Pass v. Johnson," (July 19, 2024). https://crsreports.congress.gov/product/pdf/LSB/LSB11203#:~:text=in%20City%20of%20Grants%20Pass%20v.,-Johnson&text=Johnson%2C%20holding%20that%20laws%20that,%E2%80%9Ccruel%20and%20unusual%E2%80%9D%20punishments.

21 For the capitalist dimension of public parks, see Kevin Loughran, "Parks for Profit: The High Line, Growth Machines, and the Uneven Development of Urban Public Spaces," *City & Community* 13, no. 1 (2014), https://doi.org/10.1111/cico.12050; Kevin Loughran, *Parks for Profit: Selling Nature in the City* (Columbia University Press, 2022). For the eroding democratic ideal of public parks, see David J. Madden, "Revisiting the end of public space: Assembling the public in an urban park," *City & Community* 9, no. 2 (2010); Don Mitchell, "People's Park again: on the end and ends of public space," *Environment and Planning A: Economy and Space* 49, no. 3 (2017).

22 Dunbar-Ortiz, *An Indigenous Peoples' History of the United States*, 47; Loewen, *Lies My Teacher Told Me*.

23 See Zinn, *A People's History of the United States*, Chapter 4.

24 "Declaration of independence: A transcription," n.d., Retrieved on May 30, 2024 from https://www.archives.gov/founding-docs/declaration-transcript.

25 For women's property rights, see Zinn, *A People's History of the United States*, 197. For the founding fathers and slaves, see Joe R. Feagin, *Systemic Racism: A Theory of Oppression* (New York: Routledge, 2006), 11–13; "Historical Context: The Constitution and Slavery," The Gilder Lehrman Institute of American History, n.d., Retrieved on June 2, 2024 from https://www.gilderlehrman.org/history-resources/teaching-resource/historical-context-constitution-and-slavery. Kendi, *Stamped from the Beginning: The Definitive History of Racist Ideas in America*, Chapter 9. For the Constitution Convention, see Feagin and Ducey, *Elite White Men Ruling*, 14.

26 Zinn, *A People's History of the United States*, 97.

27 Zinn, *A People's History of the United States*; Joe R. Feagin and Kimberley Ducey, *Racist America: Roots, Current Realities, and Future Reparations* (Routledge, 2018).

28 Feagin and Ducey, *Elite White Men Ruling*.

29 Donna Bobbitt-Zeher, "The gender income gap and the role of education," *Sociology of education* 80, no. 1 (2007); Douglas S. Massey, *Categorically Unequal: The American Stratification System* (Russell Sage Foundation, 2007), 41–46.
30 Feagin, *Systemic Racism*.
31 KangJae Jerry Lee et al., "Social Stratification in Fishing Participation in the United States: A Multiple Hierarchy Stratification Perspective," *Journal of Leisure Research* 48, no. 3 (2016), https://doi.org/10.18666/JLR-2016-V48-I3-6544; U.S. Fish & Wildlife Service U.S. Department of the Interior, *2022 National Survey of Fishing, Hunting, and Wildlife-Associated Recreation* (2022).
32 Marx's view is particularly noticeable from his infamous work "The Communist Manifesto," written with Friedrich Engels in 1848 and the first volume of *Capital* in 1867. Karl Marx and Friedrich Engels, "The Communist Manifesto," in *Ideals and Ideologies* (Routledge, 2019); Karl Marx and Frederick Engels, *Marx & Engels Collected Works Vol 35: Karl Marx: Capital Volume 1* (London: Lawrence & Wishart, 1996).
33 Marx and Engels, *Marx & Engels Collected Works Vol 35*; David Held, *Models of Democracy* (Stanford University Press, 2006), Chapter 4.
34 Held, *Models of Democracy*, 108.
35 For capitalism and environmental destruction, see John Bellamy Foster, *Marx's Ecology: Materialism and Nature* (Monthly Review Press, 2000); John Bellamy Foster and Brett Clark, *The Robbery of Nature* (Monthly Review Press, 2018).
36 Richard D. Wolff, *Understanding Marxism* (Democracy at Work, 2018), 18.
37 Held, *Models of Democracy*, Chapter 4; Richard D. Wolff, *Democracy at Work: A Cure for Capitalism* (Haymarket Books, 2012).
38 Held, *Models of Democracy*, Chapter 4; Wolff, *Democracy at Work*.
39 Wolff, *Democracy at Work*.
40 Richard D. Wolff, *Understanding Socialism* (Democracy at Work, 2019).
41 Wolff, *Understanding Socialism*.
42 Jan Rehmann, "Bernie Sanders and the hegemonic crisis of neoliberal capitalism: What next?" *Socialism and Democracy* 30, no. 3 (2016).
43 J.F. Helliwell, Layard, R., Sachs, J.D., De Neve, J.-E., Aknin, L.B., & Wang, S (eds.). *World Happiness Report* (University of Oxford: Wellbeing Research Centre, 2024). https://happiness-report.s3.amazonaws.com/2024/WHR+24.pdf.
44 Wolff, *Democracy at Work*; Wolff, *Understanding Socialism*.
45 Wolff, *Understanding Socialism*, 80.
46 Sharryn Kasmir, *The Myth of Mondragon: Cooperatives, Politics, and Working Class Life in a Basque Town* (SUNY Press, 1996); Sharryn Kasmir, "The Mondragon cooperatives and global capitalism: A critical analysis," *New Labor Forum* 25, no. 1 (2016).
47 For the Mondragón Corporation, see Wolff, *Understanding Socialism*, 82–83; Xabier Barandiaran and Javier Lezaun, "The Mondragón experience," in *The Oxford Handbook of Mutual, Co-operative, and Co-owned Business*, eds. Jonathan Michie, Joseph Blasi, and Carlo Borzaga (Oxford University Press, 2017).
48 "Cascina Falchera," n.d., Retrieved on June 1, 2024 from https://cascinafalchera.it/.
49 Regarding Cascina Falchera and the difference between common goods and public goods, see Valeria Martino and Gian Vito Zani, "Green Areas: How to Avoid the Tragedy of the Commons," *Philosophy of the City Journal* 1, no. 1 (2023).

50 George C. Edwards III, *Why the Electoral College is Bad for America* (Cambridge University Press, 2023), 68.
51 Edwards III, *Why the Electoral College is Bad for America*, 100.
52 Robert A. Dahl, *How Democratic is the American Constitution?* (Yale University Press, 2003), 67.
53 Edwards III, *Why the Electoral College is Bad for America*, Chapter 5.
54 *Electoral College Reform: Challenges and Possibilities*, ed. Gary Bugh (Routledge, 2016); Edwards III, *Why the Electoral College is Bad for America*; Alexander Keyssar, *Why Do We Still Have the Electoral College?* (Harvard University Press, 2020).
55 Marx and Engels, *Marx & Engels Collected Works Vol 35*.
56 Naomi Klein, *This Changes Everything: Capitalism vs. the Climate* (Simon and Schuster, 2015); Christopher Wright and Daniel Nyberg, *Climate Change, Capitalism, and Corporations* (Cambridge University Press, 2015).
57 The World Meteorological Organization, *State of the Global Climate 2023* (Geneva 2, Switzerland, 2024), https://library.wmo.int/viewer/68835/download?file=1347_Global-statement-2023_en.pdf&type=pdf&navigator=1.
58 John T. Hardy, *Climate Change: Causes, Effects, and Solutions* (John Wiley & Sons, 2003).
59 Drew Shindell et al., "The effects of heat exposure on human mortality throughout the United States," *GeoHealth* 4, no. 4 (2020).
60 William J. Ripple et al., "The 2024 state of the climate report: Perilous times on planet Earth," *BioScience* (2024): 1.
61 Foster, *Marx's Ecology*; Foster and Clark, *The Robbery of Nature*.
62 William J. Ripple et al., "World scientists' warning of a climate emergency," *BioScience* 70, no. 1 (2020); Ripple et al., "The 2024 state of the climate report: Perilous times on planet Earth."

Index

Note: Page numbers in *italics* indicate figures, **bold** indicate tables in the text, and references following "n" refer notes.

11th Street Bridge Park 90

Abrams, W. P. 40
Adams, J. Q. 39
Adirondack Forest Preserve 44–5, 49, 93, 95
affinity groups, outdoor recreation 105
African Americans: in Baltimore 24; Black resorts 50; Black sport organizations 50; contribution to park development 102–3; discrimination in parks 4, 47–9, 78; exclusion and disfranchisement 52–3; leisure and park access strategies 50–1; Negro Election Day 16; outdoor affinity groups 105; as park rangers 103; racial segregation 24, 47; resistance and struggles 25, 50–1, 103, 106; Seneca Village 21; state parks for 2, 47–50; Tulsa-Greenwood Race Massacre 51–2
Albright, H. M. 52, 57n62
American conservation movement 65, 66; elitist ideology in 66–9; leaders of 91
American Frontier 64–5, 66
American public parks 2, 128; behaviors 22, 23, 24; beneficiaries of 3; benefits of 2–3, 24; capitalism 118–9; 128–9; climate change 128–9, 130; closure 25–6, 96; colonialism 35–7; commercialization 27, 97; contemporary disparities 26–28; contradictions 4–5; democracy 116–7, 128–9; democratic ideal 13–14; design 94; development, hidden motives 20, 27, 30; elite motivations and influence 20, 23; elitism, racism, and sexism 120–22, 130; exclusion in 23–4; founding ideals 91–2; gentrification 27; historical evolution 1–5, 13–15, 23, 26, 36–7; inequality 14–15; justice, struggle for 25, 116–7, 128–9; location 93–4; oppression and injustice 23–7; paradoxes of 4–5; pioneers of 91; private-public partnerships 27; privatization 25–6, 95–6; racial segregation 24–5; rules and regulations 92; as social control means 24; utopian promises 30
Antiquities Act (1906) 68
Appalachian National Park Association 75
Appalachian people 77
Arizmendiarrieta, J. M. 126
Ashley, W. H. 70

Bailey, J. 38
Beekman, J. 20
Belt Line project 89–90
Bierstadt, A. 42
Bishop, H. 72
Bishop, S. 103
Black, D. 119
The Blackfeet 1–2, 74
Blackmar, E. 19, 21, 22
Blanchard, E. 49
Blaxton, W. 15–16
Boling, J. 41
Bonneville, B. 40

136   Index

Booker T. Washington State Park 95
Boston Common 14, 15; class conflict 17–18; historical transformation 15–18; as multipurpose space 16; racial inequality in 16; Shawmut Peninsula 15–16; socioeconomic divide 17; transition from town to city 17–18
Bozeman, J. 70, 71
Bransford, Masterson "Mat" 103
Bransford, Matt 103
Bransford, N. 103
Bransford, Z. 103
Bridger, J. 70
Brown, J. W. 13
Buder Park 25, 95
Bunnell, L. H. 41

Cammerer, A. B. 48, 76
Cammeron, M. 96
Campbell, D. G. 39
capitalism: and climate change 128–30; in Marxist tradition 122–4; systemic park injustice contribution 118–20
Caro, R. 28
Carson, A. C. 75, 77
Carson, W. E. 75
Cascina Falchera 127
Catlin, G. 62, 63
Cedar Hill State Park 97
Central Park: class boundaries 22; class conflicts 22–3; construction 22; cost on New Yorkers 21; creation of sports spaces in 102–3; Jones Wood plan 19–20; as landscaped natural space 14–15; motives for 19–21; Olmsted's vision 13, 22–3, 91; park behaviors 22; people displacement 20–1; regulations and rules 22, 92; Seneca Village demolition 21
City of Grants Pass v. Johnson case 119–20
Civilian Conservation Corps (CCC) program 47–9, 61
climate change 128–9, 130
Cole, T. 65
colonialism 3; and capitalism 117–20; colonial conquests 36, 117–8; colonial ideologies 118, 120; Columbus' barbarian method 36; European 15–18; settler 35–40
Colter, J. 69–70
Columbus, C.: colonial conquests 36, 118; monument 104

commercialization 27–28, 97–8; Niagara Falls 64; Yellowstone National Park 71–2; Yosemite 41–3
Commission on Conservation and Development (CCD) 75
common goods 127
commons 14
communism 123–5
community parks 14–15
community: participation 100–101; unfair input 90
Community Benefits Agreements (CBAs) 99–100
Community Benefits Funds (CBFs) 100
Confederate monuments 96–7, 103–4
Conness, J. 42, 43
conservationists 66–9
Cooke, J. 71
Coolidge, C. 74
Creeks 37–40; *see also* Indian Springs State Park
Cronon, W. 70

Dahl, R. A. 127
Darling, E. 50
Darst, J. 96
Davis, A. 74
Davis, W. P. 74
Deloria, V. 37
DeMallie, R. J. 37
democratic: access in parks 46–7, 51; parks 116–7, 128–9; socialism 125; voting system 127–8; workplaces 126–7
discriminatory federal policies 96
discriminatory laws 95; discriminatory federal policies 96; Jim Crow 4, 13, 47, 49–51, 52, 53, 95; "separate but equal" doctrine 4, 47, 51
disinvestments 96
displacement 1–2, 18–23, 61–2, 93, 94; Appalachian residents 75–7; Central Park 20–1; of Indigenous peoples 15, 70–71, 81n18; of marginalized communities 27; Yellowstone 70–71
Doctrine of Discovery 117–8
Douglass, F. 24, 106
Downing, A. J. 19, 22
dual-use parks 47, 94
Ducey, K. 119
Dunbar-Ortiz, R. 117, 120
Dunlap, G. 37

Eisenhower, D. D. 77
elitism 66–9; 91–2, 120–22

Emerson, R. W. 22, 65
encroachments *see* land dispossession
ethnic cleansing 35–40
exclusion: and elitism 91–2; exclusionary practices 92; of poor and people of color 23–6; in state parks 51–3; symbolic exclusion 96–7

Fairground Park Riot 95
Faulkner, W. J. 34
Feagin, J. R. 139
Fechner, R. 48
Fernandez, M. 94–5
Ferris, W. A. 70
Floyd, G. 103
Folsom-Cook-Peterson expedition 63, 69
Folsom, D. E. 63, 71
Fort Bridger Treaty (1868) 73
Foster, W. 17
Franklin, B. 128
Franklin D. Roosevelt (FDR) 61, 77, 104, 124

General Election Day *see* Negro Election Day
gentrification 89; environmental 4; green 27, 94, 98–99
Glacier National Park 61–2
Gorges, R. 15
Grant, M. 67
grants 99
Grant, U. S. 72
Great Smoky Mountains National Park (GSMNP) 62, 74; Appalachians displacement 76–7; land acquisition for 75
Greeley, H. 42
green gentrification 27, 94, 98–99; *see also* displacement
greenspace: "green space paradox" 27; hidden cost of 1–6; impact of systemic oppression 26–7
"greensplaining" 27, 94–5
Groom, H. H. 25

Halladay, A. 104
Hall, R. 61, 62
Haque-Hausrath, K. 104
Harding, W. L. 46
Hawkins, S. 39
Hayden, F. V. 71–2
Heckscher State Park 50
Hedges, C. 63
Henry, A. 70

Hesser, J. Z. 1, 2
High Line 27
Hill Park 97
Hine, D. 50
Hitler, A. 67
Hoover, H. C. 77
Hornaday, W. T. 67–8
Hot Springs National Reservation 63
housing programs, affordable 98–9
Humboldt Park 89
Hutchings, J. M. 42

Ickes, H. L. 103
Indian Springs State Park 35, 37–40; Chief William McIntosh 38–9; discovery of 37; Treaty of Indian Springs (1821) 39; Treaty of Washington (1826) 39–40, 55n28
Indigenous: Ahwahneechee 40, 41; co-management 105–6; criminalization of park use 73, 92; displacement 15, 70–71, 75–7, 81n18; erasure of histories 3, 36; ethnic cleansing against 35–6; heritages for tourism marketing 74; manipulative treaties against 37; military campaigns against 2; Osh Kosh Camp 94; petition and federal protection 43–4; restrictions on Indigenous activities 73; Roosevelt considerations on 69; Seneca Village 21; Smoky residents 76; Yellowstone 69
Informal Green Space (IGS) 101–2
injustice *see* park injustice

Jacobs, J. 70
Jacoby, K. 92
Jefferson, T. 118, 121
Jensen, J. 47
Jim Crow 4, 13, 47, 49–51, 52, 53, 95
Johnson, A. 89
Johnson, G. 119
Johnson, R. U. 43
Johnston, F. T. 48
Jones Lake State Park 2
Jones Wood plan 19–20

Kahrl, A. 96
Kaplan, R. D. 118
Kelley, W. D. 71
King, T. S. 42
Ku Klux Klan 25, 50, 95

La Casas, B. de 36, 131n16
Land and Water Conservation Fund Act 96

Land Back Movement (LBM) 105–6
land dispossession 37; Appalachians and Indigenous peoples 75–6; in Baltimore 24; betrayal of treaties 37; Central Park 20–1; *City of Grants Pass v. Johnson case* 119–20; Creek Nation 38–9; Seneca Village 21; wars and massacres 37; Yellowstone 69–74; Yosemite 40–4; *see also* displacement
Lane, F. K. 45, 57n62
Legal Defense and Educational Fund 51
Letters and Notes on the Manners, Customs, and Condition of the North American Indian (Catlin) 62
Lewis, W. 44
Lincoln, A. 43
Loewen, J. 36, 97, 120
Logan, J. 119–20
Loudon, J. C. 91
Loughran, K. 28, 98
Lyons, A. J. 21
Lyons, M. J. 21

Mackinac Island State Park 45, 57n57
Madison, J. 128
Mammoth Cave National Park 103
Manning, W. H. 25
Mariposa Big Tree Grove 35
Mariposa Estate 92
Mariposa Indian War 40
Marshall, T. 50
Marx, K. 122–5, 128, 133n32
Mather, S. T. 45–6, 74, 57n62
McDougal, J. 41
McIntosh, W. 38–9
McKay, R. B. 48
McNutt, P. V. 49
Meagher, T. F. 71
Memorial to the Confederate Dead in Forest Park (St. Louis) 104
Mendez de Canzo, G. 14
Meriwether, J. 39
Miles, N. A. 72, 77
Miller, A. 45
Minturn, A. M. W. 19
Minturn, R. B. 19
Mondragón Corporation 126–7
Montgomery Bell Recreational Demonstration Area 34–5
monument building 96–7
Moore, T. 41
Moses, R. 28
Mount Mitchell State Park 47

Mount Rushmore National Memorial 68
Mowatt, R. A. 102
Muir, J. 43
Myrdal, G. 48

National Conference on State Parks (NCSP) 34, 46; mission of 47
national parks 2–3, 61; accessibility 47; American conservation movement 65, 66–9; in Appalachians 74–7; capitalist roots 72; commercialization 97–8; conservation for profits 69–74; conservation cost 78–9; conservation to displacement 61–2; demographic divide 78; environmental destruction 64–6; exclusivity of access 78; focus of 46; imperialism emblems 3; Mather's promotion of 45–6; origins and complexities of 62–4; park rangers in 93; racial and ethnic disparity 78; and racialized ideologies 66–9; regulations 92–3; symbol of oppression 62; Washburn-Langford-Doane Expedition 63; White conservation elites 66–9, 91
National Park Service (NPS) 34–5; 45, 46, 48, 64, 76, 99, 105–6
National Park Service Organic Act (1916) 64, 78–9
Negro Election Day (NED) 16
Nettleton, A. B. 71
New York City: Department of Parks 28; emergence of urban parks in 18–19
New York Zoological Society (NYZS) 67
Nez Perce War 72; invalidity of Nez Perce Treaty (1863) 83n80
Niagara Falls 64–5
Norris, P. 73

O'Brien, W. 47, 48
Olmsted, F. L. 13, 22, 23, 25, 28, 42, 91, 92
Open Space Land Program 96
Opothle Yoholo 39
oppression 23–6, 91; Appalachian mountain residents 76; impact on greenspace 26–7; national parks as symbols of 62; in state parks 51–3; and tourism marketing 74; Yellowstone-area tribes 74

Osborn, H. F. 67
Osborn, W. H. 67
Osh Kosh Camp 94
Otis, H. G. 17
Our Vanishing Wild Life (Hornaday) 68
Outdoor Recreation Legacy Partnership (ORLP) 99

park gentrification *see* green gentrification
park injustice 23, 89–90; commercialization 27–28; privatization 25–6, 27–28; racial segregation 24–5; redlining 26–7; struggle for racial justice in 25; systemic oppression impact 26–7; *see also* systemic park injustice
park injustice, countering 90, 98, 106–7; addressing racial inequality 102; affordable housing programs 98–9; challenging colonial legacies 104–5; coalitions and partnerships 101; Community Benefits Agreements 99–100; Community Benefits Funds 100; community participation 100–101; creating informal and smaller parks 101–2; diversifying workforce 102; Douglass' message 106–7; equitable greening strategy 101–2; grants and financial support programs 99; Land Back Movement 105–6; marginalized communities 102–3; outdoor recreation affinity groups 105; preventing green gentrification 98–9; renaming and removing Confederate monuments 103–4
The Passing of the Great Race (Grant) 67
Paxton, J. 91
Payne, J. B. 46
Peay, A. 75
Plaza de la Constitución (Plaza de Armas) 14
Plessy, H. 47, 57n77; *Plessy v. Ferguson* 47
Poletti, C. 50
policing 93
Pollock, G. F. 74
post-industrial parks 27–28
Powell, M. 69
Powell, S. 1, 2
The Power Broker (Caro) 28

Preston Gardens Park 24
Preston, J. H. 24
privatization 25–6, 27–28; 95–6
public parks *see* American public parks

racism: in American Conservation Movement 66–9; and class segregation 94; and elitism 91–2, 120–2; in Northern state parks 49–50; oppression 51–3; park disparity 48
Rawson, M. 16, 17
Ray, C. B. 21
Raymond, I. W. 42
Recreational Demonstration Areas (RDAs) 34–5
Revolutionary War 120
Robert E. Lee Park 104
Robinson, R. C. 48
Roof, D. 103
Roosevelt, F. D *see* Franklin D. Roosevelt
Roosevelt, T. 61, 67, 68
Rosenzweig, R. 19, 21, 22
Runte, A. 64
Russell, O. 70
Rutherford, M. F. 49

Sanders, B. 125
Savage, J. D. 40–1
Schullery, P. 70
Seashore State Park 51
Seneca Village 21
"separate but equal" law 4, 47, 51
Sequoia National Park 64, 93, 103
settler colonialism 3, 15–16; 35–40
Sharik, T. 102
Shawmut Peninsula 15–16
Shenandoah National Park (SNP) 62, 74; Association 75; land acquisition for 75; removal of Appalachian people 76–7
Shurtleff, N. 18
slavery 16, 97, 119, 121, 128
socialism 123–5; in business and public management 126–7; democratic socialism 125; potential of 125–7; relation with U.S political system 124; socialism-oriented countries 125
South Carolina State Parks 34
Spence, M. 44
state parks 2, 34; for African Americans 47–53; democratic access to 44–51; disparities and dissonance 34–5;

140 Index

legacy of violence and exclusion 51–3; movement 4, 44–6, 47, 53; origins of 35; paradox of 4; racial discrimination 46–51; racial oppression 51–3; settler colonialism and ethnic cleansing 35–40; unequal access and hidden inequities 34–5; visitor statistics 52–3
Stegner, W. 77, 78
Stewart, W. D. 70
Sullinger, E. L. 50
systemic park injustice 91; closure 96; colonialism and capitalism 117–20; commercialization 97–8; criminalization of park use 92; discriminatory laws and customs 95; disenfranchisement 93, 94; disinvestments 96; elitism, racism, and sexism 91–2, 122; exclusion 91–2; fight against 106–7; founding ideals of public parks 91–2 "greensplaining" 94–5; location 93–4; marginalizing communities 94, 96, 97; naming and monument building 96–7; origin of 117; park features and segregation 94; policing and surveillance 93; privatization 95–6; rules and regulations 92; symbolic exclusion 96–7; unfair community 90; white middle-class dominance 91–2; white terrorism 95; *see also* park injustice
systemic racism 121–2

Tenaya, Chief 41
Thomson, C. 44
Thoreau, H. D. 65
Treaty of Indian Springs (1821) 38–40
Treaty of Washington (1826) 39–40, 55n28
Trent, W. J., Jr. 103
Troup, G. M. 38, 39
Tulsa-Greenwood Race Massacre 51–2, 53
Turner, L. 49
Turtle Creek Park 104
Tyson, L. 75–6

urban parks: Boston Common 15–18; Central Park 18–3; economic motives 20; elite motivations behind 20; emergence in New York City 18–19; exclusion of poor and people of color 23–6; history of 2–3, 14–15
U.S. Electoral College 127–8
U.S. park movement 34, 44–51

Vance, B. 100
Van Ellis, H. 51, 52
Via, R. H. 76

Walker, J. 40
Washburn, K. 105
Watkins, C. 42
Watson, D. 37
Watt, A. 21
Weed, C. L. 42
White Calf, Chief 1
White conservation elites 91–2; elitism, racism, and sexism of 120–22; White dominance 102
White supremacy 3, 66, 68, 104
White terrorism 95
Willis, L. 77
Wilson, W. 64
Winthrop, J. 15, 16
Wirth, C. 48, 77–8
Wolff, R. 124–5, 126
Worker Co-ops (WC) 126
Workers' Self-Directed Enterprises (WSDE) 126
Work, H. 74, 75
Wright, T. S. 21

Yellowstone 6; commercial interests 71–2; criminalizing Indigenous hunting practices 73; early explorers of 69–70; ethnocide 73; Folsom-Cook-Peterson expedition 63, 69; Indigenous displacement 70–71, 72; Indigenous groups 69; oppression 74; restrictions on Indigenous activities 73; tourism marketing campaign 74; violent history of 69; Washburn-Langford-Doane Expedition 63, 69; Yellowstone Act (1872) 72, 79; Yellowstone National Park 62, 69, 93
Yosemite 35; commercial interests and preservation 42–3; conflict to commercialization 41–2; early history of 40; Indian Field Days 4; Indigenous petition and federal protection 43–4; Mariposa Battalion 41; Mariposa Indian War 40–1; tourism development 42–3; Yosemite National Park 37, 40, 63, 64, 103; Yosemite Valley 40, 41–2; Yosemite Valley Act (1864) 35
Young, C. 103

Zinn, H. 36, 116, 121

For Product Safety Concerns and Information please contact our EU representative GPSR@taylorandfrancis.com
Taylor & Francis Verlag GmbH, Kaufingerstraße 24, 80331 München, Germany

www.ingramcontent.com/pod-product-compliance
Ingram Content Group UK Ltd.
Pitfield, Milton Keynes, MK11 3LW, UK
UKHW030828140425
457330UK00020B/268